Henry Raby is a poet, works  punk. Born and based in Yor[k] left-wing activism, anti-fascis[m].

Henry has his fingers in poet, Henry has gigged acro[ss] festival stages, cafés, librarie[s] to drunk punks and family-[friendly crowds in cities] and rural venues. In 2015 he was part of Apples and Snakes' Public Address Tour. Henry is artistic director of York's spoken word organisation Say Owt, promoting slams, open mics, scratches and workshops.

As a theatre-maker and playwright, Henry has worked with York Theatre Royal, Hull Truck and Harrogate Theatre. In 2012 he was part of the Royal Court's Young Writers' Programme and took his first solo show, *Letter to the Man (from the boy)*, to the Edinburgh Fringe with support from Pilot Theatre. Henry is co-director of Vandal Factory theatre company alongside Natalie Quatermass. Their first show, *Whatever Happened to Vandal Raptor?*, debuted in 2017 and has roots in a poem featured in this book.

He has performed his poetry at marches, occupations, rallies and fundraisers. His poetry is inspired by community and solidarity, friendship and home.

His favourite Pokémon is Gengar.

www.henryraby.com
@henry_raby
www.facebook.com/henryrabypoetry
henry@henryraby.com

Nerd Punk

Henry Raby

Burning Eye

BurningEyeBooks
Never Knowingly
Mainstream

Copyright © 2018 Henry Raby

The author asserts the moral right under the Copyright, Designs and Patents Act 1988 to be identified as the author of this work.

All rights reserved. No part of this publication may be reproduced, stored in a retrieval system, or transmitted, in any form or by any means without the prior written consent of the author, nor be otherwise circulated in any form of binding or cover other than that in which it is published and without a similar condition being imposed on the subsequent purchaser.

This edition published by Burning Eye Books 2018

www.burningeye.co.uk

@burningeyebooks

Burning Eye Books
15 West Hill, Portishead, BS20 6LG

ISBN 978-1-911570-31-8

NERD PUNK

To Cick
Noupe
Thanks x
Henry :)

CONTENTS

Up the Nerd Punks!	8
Turtles Vs Sloths	12
Boroughbridge Road	14
Buffy DVDs	16
Superman Is a Refugee	18
How to Survive a Shakespeare Play	20
Operation: Historical Ballistic Accuracy	22
Protest Hugs	24
Ode to Emma Goldman (or 'Five Books of Anarcha-Feminism')	26
The Ghost Walk Turf War	28
I'm Sorry I Missed Your Gig	30
Discount Tesco's Bunting	33
Imagine	36
Mary Sue Blues	38
Henry Raby the Brand	40
Tonight I Typed	42
Pretend You're a Dinosaur	43
Last Train Outta Beanotown	44
True Friends	45
The Cartoons Have Taken Over	46
Vandal Raptor	48
If I Can't Skank, It's Not My Revolution	49
Rise Like Lions (Snap Like Turtles)	52
Remember When It Rained?	54
My City	57

Toby the Tyrannosaurus Rex	60
Up the Nerd Punks 2	62
Five Cans of Deodorant	64
Kingdoms	67
Lost	70
Echo Chamber (Far Away in Time)	72
Nerd Punks 3D	73
One Hundred Years	76
Vision of Utopia	78
My Imposter	80
Post-Apocalypse Advisory	82
TV on Demand	84
Love Me, I'm a Millennial	86
Britain 3D	89
Three Minutes to Save the World	91
Better World	95

UP THE NERD PUNKS!

I love punk rock, I know you feel it.
From the age of sixteen I was bouncing to the ceiling
But from the age of eleven I was hunting radioactive spiders
And from the age of eight I had mastered *Age of Empires*
And since I was born I wanted to sail on a pirate ship.
This is a tribute to the nerds who don stud jackets,
The gamers who have Mohawks
And the hardcore readers into hardcore.

The only time the fist stops pumping in the air is when it rolls
    the D&D dice:
We're skanking with the Skeksis
And moshing with Sonic and the Mario brothers.
Clash City Nerfherders.
Cross-gender cosplayers make better lovers.

Nerd punk is the Ramones featuring Lion-O:
Hey-ho ThunderCats ho!
Radio radio radio CB Radio.
When I got the chiptune, I got a place to go.

The Beano, manga and zines sit on my shelf.
Does playing *Magic: The Gathering* mean I'm going Straight
    to Hell?
We're Henry Rollins the D12.
You come at us, you're gonna hurt yourself.
Punk rock is for orcs, prog rock is for elves.

I learnt about equality
From the Specials and watching *Shrek*.
We embrace all cultures,
Vulcan, Minbari and even Dalek.
Rest assured, we meet a fascist in the street,
We're gonna do more than just a Jedi mind trick.

No war but the Star Wars.
Winter is coming, bands don't tour.

ACAB: All Cyborgs Are Bugged.
No gods (except Khorne).
No masters (I will not kneel before General Zod).

Ssssssssss.
I'm singing the Clash in Parseltongue whilst chewing out a
    rhythm on my bubblegum.
Keep your steampunk and crust punk:
Up the nerd PUNKS!

What gigs do nerd punks attend?
Head down to 221B Baker Street for the squat party.
We had the sound system hooked up to *Serenity*.
We had a riot grrrl band with vocals from Lara Croft,
Bass featuring Tank Girl,
There was Turanga Leela whacking those drums.
Nerd girls to the front!
'Shut up and take my money!'
We shouted as we dropped coins into the bucket for donations.
Touring bands have to eat and buy action figures (all limited
    edition).
But afterwards, I heard a guy go, 'Yeah, they were pretty good
    for girls,'
While he didn't let his girlfriend say a word.

When I got home and went online
I saw an advert which read 'Male Gamers Only'
Next to a chained-up half-naked she-goblin
I saw a meme which said: 'Sexy Cosplayers: If she doesn't
    expect you to stare a bit, her naivety isn't your problem.'

Who's updated their privilege, who's rebooting their agency?
Who's being reduced to just part of the scenery?
Who's debugging safe spaces?
Why are non-white peoples represented as alien races?
And as much as Groot is cool, I'm still waiting for real diversity
Rather than films with a CGI talking tree.

All the nerds and punks, ask yourself:
Why is it, sometimes, our scenes seem whiter than Gandalf?

Reclaim, rebuild, reboot, retcon.
HMV will not be part of the Nerd Punk revolution.
Ha! You think it's funny?
They're turning the Rebel Alliance into money.
We are not a corner of the market to target.
We are targeting them and we're coming harder.
Our escapism is a tool we employ in nerdy defiance.

Now here's the obligatory Pokémon reference:
Either bolt to the door or take my Thunderbolt, you're in for an electric shock, these Geodude are more rock than you, you're like a Diglett beneath my shoe, if you were my last Pokémon I still wouldn't choose you. I'll send you to the grave, coast with the Ghost-types. We're harder than a bulked-up Chansey, look into my eyes, like Articuno they're icy, you think Porygon is pricey? You couldn't afford a Potion, stop causing a commotion like a beached Dewgong, I'm ten times tougher than the toughest Rhydon and here come the Egg Bomb: I'm a master of all 802 Pokémon!

Anarchy mode! Start9!
It's my job to keep nerd punk Elite Four.
Love *World of Warcraft* but oppose those who craft real war.
Make V masks yourself, not mass-produced in sweatshops.
Tear down Umbrella, Rekall, Abstergo and the Omni Consumer
    Products!
So raise your fist, or hold your palm with three fingers in the air,
For every punk who placed faith in rage and three chords,
For every nerd who found sanctuary in a gaming board,
For every outsider who refused to be assimilated,
For every introvert who subverted,
For everyone who refused to run their race
And shouldn't have to.
It's dangerous to go alone, so bring your friends, and take this:

If the sewers were good enough for the Turtles, they're good
 enough for us,
So let's celebrate an underground whilst infecting the
 mainstream above.
Up the nerd punks!

Come at me, bro, we're coming out fighting.
Make yourself as tall as the Colossus Titan.
Be like Wolverine but twice as vicious.
Make yourself as brave as Tommy Pickles.
We're looking for alternative worlds because the mechanics in
 this one are broken.
We're earth-shattering and world-builders, nerds and punk
 rockers.
Roll the dice, we're fighting.

Up the nerd punks!

TURTLES VS SLOTHS

You mess with a turtle, you lose a limb.
Your fingers are fair game.
Rough seas, shallow streams,
Turtles have one belief: The world is a strawberry
That's waiting to be snapped.
Rise and shine, grip and dine,
Always on the attack.
I'm a turtle, I go SNAP SNAP SNAP.

Sloths sleep sound, we are snoozers,
Peaceful and clingable critters.
Alert! Overtime! Disciplinary warning! Emergency!
These are not in the sloth vocabulary.
Burn the alarm clocks (if you've got the energy),
Put life on permanent snooze mode,
Dream good dreams,
Be friendly,
Hug with a good grip, nullify scorn.
I'm a sloth, I go YAWWWWN.

When life gives you lemons, you make lemonade.
When life gets in the way, you snap off its face.
I'm a turtle, I go SNAP SNAP SNAP.

When life gives you lemons, don't make lemonade;
Just sleep in all day!
I'm a sloth, I go YAWWWWN.

I swift swim, I snatch fish, give me a current that's strong, give
    me a deep sea like a reptilian love song.
I've got a helmet on my back.
I'm a turtle, I go SNAP SNAP SNAP.

I fall out of trees, I get dozy, give me a hug that's nice and
    cosy, give me a safe space, I've been sleepy since the day
    I was born.
I'm a sloth, I go YAWWWWN.

Did you know my upper shell is a carapace? Take a closer look...
    OH, I just snapped off your face.
Turtle: torpedo with fins, cheese-grater fused to a tank, fish-
    fuelled battering ram.
I'm a turtle, I go SNAP SNAP SNAP.

Did you know 10,000 years ago yawns were giant? Behold the
    ground sloth the size of an elephant!
Sloth: algae all around me, three- or four-toed take-a-load-off
    living hammock, dozing dawn till dusk and then dusk till
    dawn.
I'm a sloth, I go YAWWWWN.

You know it would never come to a war, because turtles can't
    climb trees, and sloths can't climb out of bed.
You turtles are all talk, and sloths couldn't care less.
Whether you rule the seas or sleep in trees,
Every day, make sure you snap; every night, make sure you
    dream.

BOROUGHBRIDGE ROAD

Here on Boroughbridge Road, Northallerton, North Yorkshire,
    the UK, Europe, the world, we're growing hope,
Backed up by a constant chorus of lorries and cars honking
    support
And visiting Lancaster drums putting a rhythm to our thoughts.

The people are speaking, pleading and demanding,
Raising banners and raising concerns.
The tap water catches fire and burns.

Here, in Yorkshire, we're holding white roses,
But despite us being dangerous and placard-toting
The councillors, dry inside, still voted
For fracking.

And that hits you like a drill into cracking soil.
Your throat is choked like a country road.
Your hopes flutter away like disappearing birds and bats,
Eyes stinging like they've been cracked by false air
As democracy shrugs and says, well, that's the way it works,
And so it's not just English dirt that's getting hurt.

Enough is enough.
Frack off.
It's the movement for the pun-makers.
No fracking way, frack off elsewhere, get the frack out.
Don't frack with my future.
Hit the road, Frack.

There is no second garden
Like some have second homes.
Farewell to the white rose.

There is no investing in another planet
Like investing in bank balance growth.
Farewell to the white rose.

There is no other back yard.
It's all your earth and your stones.
Farewell to the white rose.

If something smells funny
It's not just shale gas up your nose.
Plant yourself; stand up for the white rose.

There is no sustainability,
Just business, I suppose.
Plant yourself; stand up for the white rose.

Someone camps through the night.
Someone honks a horn like a scream.
Someone locks themselves to a gate.
Someone sets fire to the stream.

Somewhere, a decision is made
Where people can and cannot go.
North Yorkshire Police arrive, some stern, some smile
As they drag OAPs across a road.

Here, on Kirby Misperton Road,
Behind the police cordon:
Someone's heart is like a drill.
They hold the white rose still.

BUFFY DVDS

Cath can feel the tangle in her heart
As she adjusts the tightness of her scarf.
She checks that no one seems to be in,
Gives Hannah a nod, and so they begin.
Let rip with the spray's solid hiss,
Black gloves ensnare balled-up fists,
And before they make their getaway
They stand back and admire the bright purple A.
Hannah grabs the sex doll roughly tied
To the lads' garden wall.
And this simple act
Feels like finally being on the counter-attack.
Hannah says (through her scarf),
'If you want to start a revolution, start feeling human.
Stop acting like property and you'll never be stolen.'
Well, the campus just typed and talked
About 'overreaction' and 'militant force'.
Cath was told bluntly, 'Theft is theft,'
But this didn't make her feel any less depressed
Than when every single advert tells her how to look and love
Or the bulls who banter words thick like clubs
Or the wolves at the bar who prowl for blood
Or the bouncer who said, 'Calm down, love.'
So she accepts tablets like tiny pockets of sanctuary.
Her and Hannah set aside Sunday and they watch *Buffy* DVDs.
Hannah's stitches still hurt; instead of resting she's been up all night
Debating with a bunch of boring, predictive gits
Who hide behind emoticons and clicks,
Obsessed with the whereabouts of her dick.
But she always types:
If you want to start a revolution, start feeling human.
Stop acting like property and you'll never be stolen.
Now Cath is driving: shoe. Pedal. Floor.
Their escape route the North Yorkshire Moors.
Her eyes scream louder than the siren of the pursuing police,
So Hannah reaches and retrieves their favourite mix CD.

Car stops, in come cops, music plays, and it rocks.
Hannah says through wheezing breath
(With a copper on her chest):
'If you want to start a revolution, start feeling human.
Stop acting like property and you'll never be stolen.'
Cath never dared believe she'd allow herself to feel this scared.
We all feel that grip tighten
But we can all sing louder than sirens.

SUPERMAN IS A REFUGEE

I have the power!

As a teenager, my main priority with adolescent evolution was an attempt to develop superhuman abilities.

I used to try and stick to my bedroom wall, hold out my hand to summon energy bolts or try and move things with my mind.

It did not take long to establish I had not developed mutant powers.

At school, I would imagine what it would be like if Oaklands Secondary School was Hogwarts, with magic instead of design technology.

Assuming my genetics just gave me bad acne, a funny walk and the inability to grow a proper beard, I settled on waiting for an irradiated animal, cosmic rays or gamma radiation, because obviously they're all safe, right?

So far, I'm still waiting.

I waited for a wise, elderly man to come and reveal my place in a master plan involving lightsabres, magic rings or a sword in some stone, because obviously I must be important, right?

I'm still waiting.

But I have a power with language. Wherever I go in the world, my English tongue will be enough.

When I travel, customs will never suspect I am secretly a would-be world-conquering mastermind, despite most supervillains, like superheroes, being white men.

In books, television, films, I see myself. In the history books, the characters on television, the crew of films. The lawmakers. I see myself.

No one has ever mistaken me for a bird, or a plane.

For the record, I've always got onto planes willingly.

But the ghost of Jimmy Mubenga doesn't need wings.

I suspect everyone has a secret identity. I suspect the reason phone boxes still exist is we all need to take a moment to shelter in a private space as we prepare ourselves for the outside world full of buildings we can't leap over, locomotives more powerful than us and bullets we can't outrun.

For the record, I've never had to outrun a bullet.

But the ghost of Jean Charles de Menezes is outpacing tube trains.

I am not a shapeshifter, and no one will ever confuse, or challenge, my gender. I will probably never be the object of a song. I will probably never be the object of a joke. I will probably never be the subject for an insulting Channel 4 documentary. *My Big Fat Nerd Punk Poet Wedding.*

I pray the ghost of Vikki Thompson doesn't haunt her all-male prison.

Superman is a refugee, escaping destruction and seeking sanctuary. It's just a lucky coincidence he's from the western side of Krypton.

Even if Batman's parents weren't murdered, he'd still be using his wealth to hurt people with mental illnesses.

And this may not be a superpower, but it is the power of privilege.

My career aspirations were, and still are, pirate, ninja and/or dinosaur. But if I was pumped full of chemicals at the behest of my government to fight for truth and justice as a super-soldier, I would petition my commanding officer to grant me the freedom not to wear my country's flag on my costume – sorry, uniform.

The flag of my country appears on my passport holder, the default setting for languages, hoodies, keyrings, pencil sharpeners, teddy bears, border control uniforms, bombs and the drones which drop them.

HOW TO SURVIVE A SHAKESPEARE PLAY

Thou know'st 'tis common; all that lives must die,
Passing through nature to eternity.

Henry Raby's Top Tips for How to Survive a Shakespeare Play:

Don't fall asleep.

If you find your love seemingly dead, maybe wait a few seconds. Give it a minute. Don't rush into anything. Suicide might be an excuse, but it's not a solution: *We have no friend. But resolution, and the briefest end.*

Don't antagonise the antagonist. The king of cats scratches back. If you are the king of cats, be careful who you stab, because that might come back to bite you in the…

Asps are dangerous snakes and should be left well alone.

Where to start when monologuing in Denmark? Unless you're totally certain, don't hide behind curtains. Don't go for a dip, forget the revenge trip, don't follow the instruction to the letter, don't use poison, don't raise a toast: basically don't listen to ghosts.

Sometimes you're in too deep, you're just right up to your neck in it.

If you find yourself in the Tower of London, there's not much more that can be done, but on the plus side you might end your mortal time with one last mouthful of sweet wine.

I have no words; my voice is in my sword. Make sure you're certain of winning wars; not everyone wants to trade your kingdom for their horse.

I bear a charmed life, which must not yield to one of woman born! Impressive boast, but (as we established) don't listen to ghost(ly being)s.

See, when you're told by a seer, 'Beware the Ides of March,' you'd better see sense and hear the seer.

If you make enemies you'll go down hard. They'll make their move at a wedding… and then the Lannisters send their regards…

Sorry, I got a bit lost. *Confusion now hath made his masterpiece.*

This doesn't belong on some dusty shelf; this should be splattered across stages. When the arts and theatres get cut, we bleed, but we're used to it. We're the ones who weave a tapestry of tragedy, but must not become a casualty of austerity.

How to keep Shakespeare characters alive? Don't fall asleep. Stay awake.

This is our heritage of gory glorious English slaughter, as you can see. Or maybe not if you're Gloucester…

So what have we learnt to keep a handle on that brief candle?
Don't engage in pillow talk, try not to sleepwalk.
Here's a pie! No, thanks, I'll stick to bread.
Tighten up! Don't lose your head!
Sweet prince? Mind the edge!
King of Scotland? Sleep in another bed.
Let's be clear:
In Bohemia beware of bears.
If you're a fool, dry yourself off, pack your bags and get out, because mad kings aren't good company for clowns.

If you're a poet, beware of crowds

The rest is silence.

OPERATION: HISTORICAL BALLISTIC ACCURACY

'The past is a foreign country: they do things differently there.'
When the governments of the world realised this they got scared.
They had brought peace and stability to the present, but people still lived in the past.
So (without much hesitation) a new legislation was passed.
If yesterday wouldn't comply with free world democracy
Then the twenty-first century would wage a war with history.
Funds were redirected, conscription introduced and the public all agreed.
The prime minister announced: 'We'll spend our money on a giant time machine!
If today is a safe world, then the past must be unsafe.
It's clearly full of dictators and terrorists, so let's hurry up and invade!'
They dispatched aircraft carriers to intercept Viking longboats,
Sent in paratroopers to bypass medieval castle moats.
Even the Mongol army surrendered when faced with cluster bombs,
While biological weapons reduced the Hundred Years' War to a mere day long.
Bazookas proved effective when used at Agincourt
And armoured tanks changed the course of the American Civil War.
The Trojan War was over in the blink of an eye,
Thanks to Agent Orange spreading like wildfire.
Spanish galleons sunk by submarines,
Drones drowned out the Aztec screams.
And, it just so happened, the past also had oil
And land to develop, gas and unpolluted soil,
But that was purely coincidental, hardly worth mentioning.
So the governments declared: 'Victory over history, time for celebration!'
But even after they'd executed every historical dictator,
Carved up nations, banned languages, displaced peoples,
The past still haunted the present like a spectre.
No matter how many history books got rewritten

Or people objectively branded as heroes or villains
The governments of the free world still could not conquer the past,
So they came up with one, final, decisive task.
They sexed up a dossier and came to a stalwart decision.
They called in one final strike, gave a plucky youngster a mission.
Big Business pushed for it, and the military generals all planned
To blow up the Big Bang with an even bigger bang!
The media ran with the title: 'The ultimate WMD
Is at the very beginning of all time and history.'
No more history repeating, no more sins of the past to manage,
And if it causes the destruction of life, time and reality, well, it's unfortunate collateral damage.
'The past is a foreign country: they do things differently there,'
And it's when the past catches up the governments of the world get scared.

PROTEST HUGS

Do you remember at the first protest, when our eyes met like battle lines
And as society was in decline, I knew that everything would work out just fine?
I caught your name above the chants; beneath the banner we held hands
And added to our growing list of demands.
Bulletproof glass couldn't stop us from stealing a kiss.
We made it into the newspapers, but it wasn't in the classified lists,
And when they tell us to grow up we'll reply simply this:
We're not apathetic, and neither are we thugs.
We're fuelled by the power of protest hugs.
I remember as we built the barricades I turned to you to say,
'I'm glad there was no other way.'
I'm glad that occupations occupied our time,
That we dated on picket lines.
Forget the factions; we were a living, breathing protest Valentine.
We pitched our tent in the name of peace and fought pitched battles with the police
And you replaced the riot squads in my dreams.
Because we're not apathetic, and neither are we thugs.
We're fuelled by the power of protest hugs.
And I always imagined if the people rose up in love and anger,
A million voices, not one stranger, we'd be shouting loudest in the centre.
In the middle of the throng as I ducked a petrol bomb we'd have a protest cuddle.
So I'd say to people: make sure your banner is unfurled, no question we can change this world,
Because mine was changed by just one person.
Because we're not apathetic, and neither are we thugs.
We're fuelled by the power of protest hugs.
People said it wouldn't last, fires die when they burn too fast
And it wouldn't be just our clothes to turn black,
And I remember the last protest, at you by me,
In the rain so no one could see the tears on our cheeks.

And now we meet again after many years, I swear I won't shed any more tears
Because I dehydrated myself on the barricades we built to defend what we hold dear.
Because we're not apathetic, and neither are we thugs.
We're fuelled by the power of protest hugs.

ODE TO EMMA GOLDMAN (OR 'FIVE BOOKS OF ANARCHA-FEMINISM')

There have always been (and will always be) young people who question the workings of the world, raging against the sweet ration and battling against the injustice of bedtime.

In 1869 a girl was born into the Russian Empire's poverty. Despite the threat of pogroms, school books burnt, brutality and beatings, Emma still spoke back.

Arriving in New York, Emma discovered the mechanisation of modern life in the American system, where the wage slavery of the day isn't a parent's helping hand; it's a master's balled fist.

Emma became an anarchist, realising all men and women are property in the eyes of the capitalist state, patriotism assumes the world is divided by iron gates, religion trains slaves and marriage makes slaves.

Emma's sentences were dipped deep in gasoline. Hearing her speak of revolution was a revelation; if your ears were a nation then your ear drum would be banging the beat for freedom.

She cooked her speeches and writing with the insight of Emerson, Ibsen and Wilde, and when she spoke it was with the celebration of being alive. Emma spoke out.

Now, Emma was no proto-hippie; she was a celebrity of anarchy. The papers named her Red Emma: the most dangerous woman in America. She was arrested for her part in an assassination attempt and argued the need for propaganda of the deed.

Emma spoke out free love, sex worker rights, better birth control and homosexual liberty at the turn of the century. *Man can conquer nations, but his armies cannot conquer love*, she wrote, because love is a hope that topples the king from his throne.

Emma travelled to Soviet Russia and was disillusioned with the Bolshevik state responsible for the annihilation of the most fundamental values, both human and revolutionary. Others argued the end justifies the means, but in her eyes terror must never be institutionalised.

'If I cannot dance to it, it's not my revolution!' Her famous quote came from being told her frivolous dancing would only hurt the cause. If anyone tells you this, don't pause; just keep dancing or singing or riding the fairground rides.

Every tiny act of expression forms a join-the-dots worldwide constellation of rebellion. Like the arms that lock tight outside NATO summits.

So why remember Red Emma? Like a punk rock Pussy Riot party, let's look beyond equal pay to a day when price tag society no longer makes us property, there is no binding packaging to love and no hierarchy to label us. The only competitive culture I want is a dancing competition.

What else are we fighting for, if not the freedom to dance until the sun is dawning without the fear of landlords calling or the harsh grasp of work the next morning?

THE GHOST WALK TURF WAR

It happened so long ago, no one really remembers any more
What exactly everything kicked off the Ghost Walk Turf War.
In my town you could find spooky stories galore
About ghosts and ghouls before the Ghost Walk Turf War.
Then men realised they could make money leading tours
Showing people the sites, before the Ghost Walk Turf War.
Things were peaceful, for a while, as tourists would explore
The places haunted with dark histories and mysteries.
The number of tours and walks became more and more,
Too many tours, too much competition, tensions soared
And so began the Ghost Walk Turf War.
Tour guides would send trained ravens as spies.
Tour guides used their costumes to hide sharpened knives.
Tour guides would find new allies and swap sides.
Tour guides would fling flyers into their rivals' eyes.
Tour guides would engage in storytelling drive-bys.
It's the ghost walk turf war, nobody gets out alive, nobody
    survives telling stories about how the dead decide to rise
    and scare the living. We're just making a living and a killing.
Meanwhile the ghosts just wanted to rest in peace,
Not receive an RRP,
Wanted to haunt their old homes without the chorus of cameras,
So these spooks found anger.
This was a time for action, not ghostly talk,
So they all upped and went on a real ghost walk.
Off on a journey with the banshee, these haunters wander out
    the walls, expect the spectre to saunter, maids so sombre,
    clanking armoured knights flanked by poltergeists. There's
    creatures of the night, ghouls in two-by-twos and roaming
    Roman phantoms. This parade of wraiths from the grave is
    headed by headless horsemen and, bringing up the rear,
    fallen Viking swordsmen. In the middle maybe you could
    see the shady Grey Lady slowly fading into the mist so hazy.
    The Barghast is last, one last blood-curdling scream and
    then… it leaves…
You'd think with all the ancient ghosts leaving town
The Ghost Walk Turf War would kind of die down

But some industries you can't kill so easily
And all those deceased resulting from the Turf War
Simply became more attractions for the survivors' tours!
I don't live in the plastic peace of a museum piece.
My city is not preserved under glass.
Bring this city to life today, not haunted by the past.
You'd be a fool to ignore
The lessons of the Ghost Walk Turf War.

I'M SORRY I MISSED YOUR GIG

I'm sorry I missed your gig.
I was tired, the headache struck.
I didn't have enough cash for the bus.
The gig was far too expensive, it was far too far.
I can't afford the drinks they sell at the bar.
I don't drink, so it feels no good
To sip water in a glugging pub.
I was unwell, I broke my arm, my spine, my leg.
I had a better time wrapped up in bed.
Loud music isn't good for my health.
This Netflix series won't watch itself.
I'm sorry I missed your gig.
I'm washing my hair.
I'm fighting a bear.
I'm washing my bear's hair.
To be honest: I don't really care.
To be honest: I'm hungover. I was drunk.
To be frank: I don't like the genre.
I'm not a fan of the venue's sound.
I was on a comedown.
My parents say I'm not allowed.
Was at a different gig.
Got my dates muddled up.
Turned up at the wrong venue on the wrong day in the wrong
    year.
I'm sorry I missed your gig.
It's the season premiere of *Game of Thrones*.
It's the season finale of *Game of Thrones*.
Honestly, I'm just going to stay in and rewatch *Game of
Thrones*.
I was playing Bill Sykes in *Oliver*.
It's up a flight of stairs.
It's up one step.
I can't stand up for too long.
Eurovision's on.
I'm sorry I missed your gig.
I'm off to the Edinburgh Fringe the next day.

I don't support pay to play.
All the money goes into someone else's wallet.
Is that really punk, to line someone else's pocket?
I'm really busy. I'm out of the country.
My friend's going through a terrible time.
Now don't whine, I've seen you plenty of times.
Family emergency was a matter of urgency.
I might be misgendered. I might be attacked.
It's not a safe neighbourhood if you're Asian or black.
It's a space bulging with macho bros
Obsessed with my clothes.
It's a pretty sexist zone.
You may not like to hear it,
But your gig is transphobic.
I'm sorry I missed your gig.
Didn't know. Lost my phone. Off social media.
To be honest, you didn't need me, did you?
I was working. I had work the next day.
I've grown up, for goodness' sake.
I'm an adult now.
Gigs are what the kids do.
I needed a massive poo.
I'm sorry I missed your gig.
Rain. Snow. Flood.
Broken bike.
Guide dog on strike.
I thought someone told ya? I was in a coma.
Parents won't drive me.
Erm, actually
It doesn't fit my new identity.
I'm sorry I missed your gig.
The venue owner is a dickhead.
The promoter is a dickhead.
The sound engineer is a dickhead.
The audience are dickheads.
The acts are dickheads.
You're a dickhead.

So I'm sorry I missed your gig.
I made an error in looking in the mirror
And I wanted to change my hair, my clothes, my face,
My bones, my blood, my brain.
I'm going nowhere, I'm out of place,
Never getting past the 'hi' stage.
I wish fitting in was part of a routine.
I wish I could rescript this scene.
I wish it was tomorrow morning
And tonight was fun but done.
I wish I could be them, and I wish this could end,
So I hang my face with my T-shirt to the side,
Start putting a beat to my apologies
And hate how they feel like lies.
I'm sorry I missed your gig.
But I know how to make them better.

DISCOUNT TESCO'S BUNTING

I go for a walk, and I point at what is mine.

That's my lamppost.
That's my cycle track.
That's my bird muck.
That's my empty packet of Walkers Salt & Vinegar flavoured crisps, blowing in the breeze.

That's my overflowing bin.
My Poundland.
My Poundworld.
My PoundEngland.

But, O, close your eyes and hear the clanking of armoured knights marching down the high street. For a time, they drown out the scattering chorus of Shakespearean quills scribbling sonnets.

Like a draining pond, Mr Toad *poop-poops* as his little car chugs along, the radio tuned to the Fab Four's greatest hits covered endlessly down the decades.

In your left ear you can hear Oliver Twist noshing a Cornish pasty. In your right ear is the dribbling snogging sound of Aunt Bessie and Mr Kipling making exceedingly good love.

This is the gift we were promised, drip-fed over time. Every Christmas, every birthday, next year, they said, it will arrive with a fanfare: DOO-DOO-DOOO.

The past is back! A return to yesteryear!

Thanks to Rupert. No, silly, not the bear.

With my eyes as closed as the ranks of Waterloo rifles, I hear the Agincourt veterans raise up banners, each with the most unEnglish of phrases, and a man dressed as Saint George (but obviously not Saint George because he was born in the Middle East) reads out:

'Refugee, multiculturalism, diversity, asylum seekers.'

There's a hiss as he says, 'Political correctness.'

The crowd bark and snarl like a kennel of Pavlov's bulldogs with the ferocity that rattles Dresden dust and spills blood in Birstall.

Remember what that English writer wrote?
'Who controls the past controls the future?'
Orwell's words leave a bitter taste in my throat.
Keep calm. Play Mumford & Sons on repeat forever.
Carry on. Watch the *Great British Bake Off*.
Keep calm. Remake *Dad's Army*.
Carry on. Hang the discount Tesco's bunting.

Or cast your Keep Calm & Carry Ons into the 5p carrier bag.

If you want your country back, visit 1381, shake hands with Wat Tyler and join the Peasants' Revolt, because our history is not a tapestry of masters, gods, kings, queens, corn laws, land laws and class wars. It's a queue of working-class solidarity.

The procession of Churchills doing the Ministry of Silly Walks is suddenly shoved to the side.

In a stroke the Diggers arrive and turn the world upside-down. The Luddites swing hammers and smash the bars across park benches.

There's the solid click of a lock as suffragettes and women from Greenham Common Peace Camp chain themselves to the library fence.

There's a scratch and hiss as matchgirls light flames.

There's the crack of batons against miners' bones in 1984.

There's the crack of bullets as a response to conscientious objection to war.

The past is never really coming back; it's just UKGold reruns on repeat.

Where is my country?

It hangs on the lips like a dispossessed mod on a white cliff.
It's found in the spit of the '77 reggae megamix.
It's in the sonnets and the music, the movements of trains, planes and ships.
It's in the colours in the fields and the washing line chatter, the sauce and the batter.
The pasties and the pastries.
It's in the deep colours of the curries.
My country's tongue is Anglo-Saxon and Norman and Roman and Latin and Huguenot and American and Australian and French and Bangladeshi and Pakistani and Jamaican and African and Polish and Czech and Romanian and…

I go for a walk, and I point at what is mine.

IMAGINE

Imagine there's a hell below us
And the demons are on the rise.
They invaded Britain and constructed an ash-black wall of rusting metal, like a *Lord of the Rings* prop. But instead of victorious Hobbits imagine snarling devils.
It divided North and South Yorkshire, crushing Doncaster into charred earth and slicing through the M1 in an attempt to scar God's Own Country.
The people of Norfolk were cornered on the sewage sections of seaside resorts, the sandier shorelines reserved for the Atlantean holiday homes.
Imagine spaceships navigating the north-east smog. In one great flash of red they zapped away Durham, Sunderland and Gateshead.
You couldn't move in the south between cities without time-travelling robots policing the roads: *Humans Must Carry ID Genetics At All Times.*
Slowly, the rest of the world forgot about Britain. The Head Vampire appeared on international television and said that additional land was annexed for his undead army to grow. He neglected to mention the land contained Manchester, Brighton and Glasgow.
'Britain does not exist,' he lied through his fangs.
The people of Essex enslaved, the people of Dorset dominated, the people of Brighton brought to heel, the people of Bristol bent the knee.
Imagine it's not even 200 years later, and the descendants of the dark wizards who dominated Dagenham tell Londoners to 'get over it' as if you can magically erase history.
So, imagine that these foes aren't inhuman, but just other human beings.
Not extraterrestrials, robots or demons. Just people.
Imagine growing up under a military occupation.
Imagine not having the right to vote, imagine having your homeland carved up, imagine displacement and demolition.
Imagine your normality is checkpoints, identity papers, night raids and detentions.

And if you even try to imagine resisting there's always the persistent lie that you are the monster.

This is no fantasy world; this is our marble dot in space; these are the frayed chapters in our long timeline.

This is the Americas, Australia, Africa, Asia and Palestine.

MARY SUE BLUES

With apologies to Roland Barthes.

The author who is penning my story has a bitterness which gives them bold deeds.
Their fingers bleed from hours and hours of research (on Buzzfeed).
If the author of her story was a writer with a deadline
Who needed to get this draft done and dry by five,
Knowing how most authors commit to their craft,
I don't think she'd exist past the first draft.

If her author sat her upon a fantasy throne, clashed through quests, stormed through battles, then maybe she'd be part of a sword-shattering mission.
She'd blow down deep into dungeons to dance in a treasure trove, feast upon insight into the human condition.
Or maybe she wouldn't be a level one mage. Within this tale on a scale wider than a dragon's… scale… she'd probably get killed on the first page.
She doesn't want to get out of bed all day, never mind lead the way for a new heroic age. Her real grasp of magics is how she bewitches herself to stop binge-watching Netflix.

If her author onomatopoeiad his pummelling panels and cheered up her life with jazzy jagged-edge *BLAMs* maybe she'd don her cape and save the day.
And on that day other women would dress just like her, much to the delight of her author's male gaze.
Her clothes are a footnote in the main story arc, merely selected from her tie-in secret war of a bedroom floor. *ZAP!* Her style is her own, not trademarked by copyrighters or reconstructed by cosplayers. With a *POW* she's all dressed now.

If her author was keen on whizzing his characters across the universe, she'd be stunned by stars, poke around on planets and trip over time.

But though she might steer the ship, she'd never be the captain.
Because in our author's galaxy, she gets picked up and taken for a ride, but our author doesn't see her as bigger on the inside.
Leaving her home is an adventure when her own head houses so many thoughts they could fill all the mind palaces of the universe. Her front door doesn't make a *swoosh* but a *click*. These thoughts feel written in an alien script.

So I guess I'm her author in a poem that doesn't even provide a blurb.
It's not Death of the Author; it's editing the word.
Tear apart the authors who smirk over tabloid articles and MRA blogs. Tear apart the authors who get offended when told they have offended someone.
The truth is page-turningly biting: when two in three women are turned away from refuge, when women are scribbled over and used, then the story needs rewriting.
The real authors turn red Hollywood carpets into deep bloodstains. They use tulips for gravestones. The real authors pen narratives of communities and solidarity.
The real authors see gender and identity not as a numbers but as a grand sweeping saga.
The real authors are playing guitars and moshing in a petrol pit.
Sword, cape or laser gun. Guitar, megaphone or mic.
We can be whatever we choose; ain't got time for the Mary Sue Blues.

HENRY RABY THE BRAND

People ask me in the street and in the board game shop and at
 the gym (yeah, right), 'Henry, what is DIY?'
And I reply…

DIY is Henry Raby patches.
Henry Raby pens, pencils, watches.
Henry Raby backpacks, handbags and satchels.
Henry Raby mugs, microwaves and garden gnomes.
Henry Raby telephones, mobile phones and megaphones.
Henry Raby Academy of Henryness
Henry Raby private health care.
Henry Raby museums supported by Henry Raby oil.
We closed the Henry Raby Theatre Royal.

It's part of life, it's part of routine,
So I'm normalising Henry Raby for an accessible brand identity.

And they asked: what is Henry Raby?
They asked: can you ever truly define Henry Raby?
Because Henry Raby belongs to us all
And you can get that quote on a poster for your bedroom wall.

Henry Raby: how do you promote yourself?
I didn't move the London; I made London move to me.
I'm like a heptadecagon and a heptakaidecagon had a baby.
 Edgy.
I don't go viral online; I go viral on VHS tape.
I send emails out. And I wait. And wait. And wait.
Wait: I feel like we're losing some essential part of what makes
 me me.
We formed an underground scene to stay true to the real
 Henry Raby.
But we stayed in bed watching YouTube all day because he's
 pretty lazy.

Remember when David Cameron said,
'We can't go on like this. I'll cut the deficit, not Henry Raby'?

Well, he lied!
So I went to the demonstration and handed out placards with my name on.
'I'm here in Parliament Square, it seems the people are angry about certain government policies... I can confirm the majority of protestors are Henry Raby.'
I launched a petition: *save Henry Raby*.
From what? A lack of signatures, of course!
What's worse: a lack of Henry or lack of Raby?
Remain in Henry, or leave Raby?
The people voted, communities ripped apart,
Then came the Chilcot Henry Raby War report.
Tony Blair lied about the Henry Raby War.
The UK chose to join the invasion of Henry Raby before all peaceful options for disarmament had been exhausted.
And I totally would have disarmed too.
I really wasn't an imminent threat.
But now I am.

I can't stand my own reflection, but we're feasting in a hall of mirrors.
When we look each other in the eye, through the blood web our own glint stares back.
Systems are still made of people, and no matter how many new apps
or memes, blogs or articles are made there are still thicker borders on the maps.
National identity can be branded, packaged and marketed by the state.
Personal identity is patched together and one to celebrate.
So what does DIY mean to you, how do you brand yourself?
What slogans do you plaster across your heart, chest and through your mouth?
Scrawny, unshaven, sweaty, shabby,
'Our next poet is Henry Rabby.'

TONIGHT I TYPED

Tonight I typed
And I didn't have enough tissues to wipe away the debris of
    spittle
And I yelled until my housemates asked me to keep the noise
    down.
They had work in the morning, and, to be fair, so did I.
In the brief moments my internet crashed
I continued to thump against the desk, just to try and relax.
I typed and typed until my fingers were simply bone
And my keyboard short-circuited as it overflowed with blood.
Only when my head was spinning from the dents
And only when I had ground my teeth into fine powder did
I hear in the distance the shareholders of BAE Systems
Wheezing to raise their wadded wallets to their puckered lips.
I heard our allies breathing a sigh of relief. Phew. No one noticed.
I heard the orphan, clearing their throat, some rubble, digging.
I heard the parents' tears trickling onto what remained.
Then I heard The Terrorist fill in another weapon resupply form
For another resupply of recruits.
No, I didn't. I couldn't hear all that. I was safe in my walls.
But I could hear the brutal cheering of politicians of all colours
United, together, in the squealing joy of a successful evening.
And as the morning sun rose, the bombs started to fall.

PRETEND YOU'RE A DINOSAUR

The world at large is far too large.
Give me four walls when things get hard.
Days can drag down stairs like gravity-dominated knuckles
And those bloody hands didn't adapt for bedtime cuddles.
In a sharp world where cuts fall like under-Blu-Tacked posters
Most of the walls are empty, feels like a desolate dry valley.
So I have one secret trick which keeps me alive, keeps me happy.
Curl up my fingers so they are razors and the air is sliced,
Duck down low, see, snatch and bite...
I pretend I'm a dinosaur!
Empty kitchen not a problem, soon be filled with other options.
Human race is going nowhere, they'll get there even faster
When we pretend to be velociraptors.
No, I don't want to go to the park today. Nice try-assic.
Can you see us? I'm cretaceous
And in this land before time jur-ass-ic's mine.
This house is my territory, been that way for all pre-history
And, what's more, unless you've got a meteor
I think I'll be just fine behind my door.
Get up and grow a pair... of claws.
Pretend you're a dinosaur.
Stick out your horns.
Pretend you're a dinosaur.
Don't eat meat? Herbivore?
You're a vegan dinosaur.
(Provided no one else is in your house)
Give a mighty roar.
Pretend you're a dinosaur.
When all's said and done
Sometimes surviving is about having fun.
When it's us versus the ice blue mammoths
It's no contest
Because we're a motherfucking T-rex,
Because yours is the Earth, and everything's that's in it
And – which is more – you'll be a dinosaur, my son.

LAST TRAIN OUTTA BEANOTOWN

I woke up one morning to the sound of my alarm clock calling me to rise and face another day.
But I couldn't help feel my world was swamped in grey.
I looked outside my window and half-expected two black and red horizontal lines streaking into forever
But instead was treated to overcast foul weather.
Did you ever get the feeling that this isn't the only world to ever exist? Once upon a time there was another world,
A world of spiky hair, red and black hooped jerseys and Abyssinian wire-haired tripe hounds.
Armouries stacked with catapults, peashooters, water pistols and an endless supply of rotten tomatoes.
Unruly, unrulable kids raised and educated on Bash Street.
Minxes, dodgers and menaces who accept authority like Lord Snooty needs charity.
So did all the dads and mums and mayors and sergeants and teachers and headmasters finally charter a master-crafted stratagem to keep these hoodlum youths at bay?
Did they realise it would turn the world so grey?
Did the Dodge Books get thrown on some sinister bonfire or are they still up in the attic, unreadable and static?
Maybe I got the last train out of Beanotown when I asked my gran to cancel my subscription and cut off my 60p addiction, to be replaced by a hunt for CDs and surreal TV.
But I still try and wake up each morning with a plan for the hijinks of the day, what scheme accompanies this twelve-panel scandal.
Fights a blur of dust and fists, puns coming thicker and faster than a combination of Fatty and Billy Whizz.
The reader's voice accompanies every story in this weekly, ever-living glory.
Our thoughts are made real in clouds hovering above our heads.
So never let the slipper have its bitter victory, never become a softy. Never quiver and simper.
Think what glorious rebellion we could achieve under the menace-manifesto of a British comics masterpiece.
I pressed snooze on my alarm clock and drifted back to sleep.

TRUE FRIENDS

You gotta know who your true friends truly are.
The only way we learn to swim is swallowing that dirty water.
It's true friends who bring on that necessary torture.
I don't trust mirrors or my own out-of-focus sight,
So we all wear the scars from far too many riotous righteous
    fights.
In tight worlds where the strong-willed mess up the weak-willed
And multi-manifestos of Truth and In-Jokes get equal billing
We'll argue and debate and slam our fists down on the table.
We'll drink until our theories become blurry, hazy and unstable.
This is what true friends are truly for, a local road in Hell
Paced upon, on occasion, to punish the sterile self.
And if I had a coin for every honest thing I've learned,
I'd buy every country so we could own the world.
But for now we'll have to deal with conquering it all
Bar by bar by bar, one pub at a time.

THE CARTOONS HAVE TAKEN OVER

I was walking through the woods and came across a city of little blue men
And a civilisation of talking peas at the bottom of the garden
And a pair of languageless puppets mere slaves to a little weed
And a parsley lion like a monster from a freakish bad dream.
A no-good wabbit is burrowing a network below
And a porky pig sneers in your ear, 'That's all, folks.'
A wily coyote is armed with weapons to blow you far
And I'm terrified of hearing the words 'KA-ME-HA-ME-HA!'
'Cause the cartoons are taking over.
'I have the power!' is yelled by a muscle-bound warrior.
He's not wearing many clothes but he's got a sword of power.
Noggin's hairy Vikings are armed with blades and axes.
They're looking for you to get in some easy practice.
My car turned out to be a Cybertron soldier
Who proceeded to transform and kick me over.
People say they can see paranoia in my eyes,
But if you look closely… there's robots in disguise,
'Cause the cartoons are taking over.
No picnic basket is safe, guarded or unattended.
Three little girls fly over, we're undefended.
In a lab a red-haired kid cooks up scientific devices
And the Jetsons and Flintstones are in a time-travel crisis.
They're led by Captain Planet and Captain Bucky O'Hare.
If you go into the sewers of mutant turtles, beware.
We've got to catch them all; I count 150.
From Bulbasaur to Mewtwo we'll make them fight for our amusement…
'Cause the cartoons have taken over
They rule the seven seas, Captains Pugwash, Silver and Hook.
There's even a talking sponge living in a pineapple if you'd care to look.
When dealing with ThunderCats I'd advise caution.
Some monstrous freaks hoard litter and garbage on Wimbledon Common.
A vile man and his dog build madcap devices to further their dastardly plan

And I think I'm going mad when I see a shapeshifting brown morphing man
'Cause the cartoons have taken over.
I'm seeing talking pigs, dogs, cats, rabbits and horses,
Veggie vampire ducks, and I say call in the armed forces.
Call in the CIA, FBI, MI5, GI Joe, MASK and the Power Rangers,
'Cause fun imagination has a glorious stranglehold on this nation.

VANDAL RAPTOR

If you thought music dinosaurs meant receding hairlines and twenty-minute drum solos then think again, because lurking in the undergrowth is a punk rock dino.

Encased in a leather jacket as tough as his scaly hide is a prehistoric monster with fire in his reptilian eyes, with a burning desire not just for cold meat but also three chords played with sharp, razor claws.

This is VANDAL RAPTOR, who tore up his Latin name in favour of punk rock fame. Spitting since he was an egg, other predators aren't even a factor; they're happy to avoid his sharp teeth, sharp studs and blunt language, 'cause VANDAL RAPTOR is a Jurassic savage.

Did you know it was all the talk a few years back when a palaeontologist shifted the earth and uncovered a skeleton with a bright red Mohawk?

The VANDAL RAPTOR was mostly found drinking cheap cider by the side of volcanoes, usually singing along to the hit anthem 'Anarchy in the Cretaceous Period'.

The only problem with dinosaurs and punk is their tiny forearms make gelling up hair really hard.

VANDAL RAPTOR put a safety pin through his tail and started a band called the Tar Pits and would have got radio play if the mainstream radio shows weren't corporate sellouts. And if radios had existed 65 million years ago.

You think the Damned released the first punk rock single? Nah, mate, VANDAL RAPTOR had a hit with 'Brontosaurus Blitz', and if cartoons were accurate then he'd be chewing on Fred Flintstone's ribs.

Just like the Exploited sang 'Punk's Not Dead', the dino-punks will stand up tall and proud and sing that dino-punk will never become extinct.

(Unless they get hit by a New Romantic meteor.)

IF I CAN'T SKANK, IT'S NOT MY REVOLUTION

Silence is a voyeur.
I want to break it with the same passion
As when bricks meet glass
And lips meet megaphones.

You have not been speaking
For fear of someone elsewhere
Recording
Secretly, in silence, at distance,
So we are paralysed on the bedroom floor
Entwined like tangled cassette tape
Waiting for dawn
Or a knock on the door.

The silence will either be broken by sirens, boots or tunes.

We examine the CDs, all mixed tracks with names such as
Picketline Emergency,
Anti-Disney,
Girls Riot Better Than Boys.
One made in 2003: *Tony & George, Put Away Your Toys.*
999 Is a Joke.
The last one is called *Anger & Hope.*

We take a chance with shuffle mode like tarot cards.
Take your shoes off, and let's dance.
If they're really spying on us,
If the police
And the government
Are really listening
And watching us,
Let's give them something to watch.
Let's defy with our feet, and the moving of our legs.
Let's be defiant from our toes to our heads.
Let's be rebels from the waist down and up.
Our feet march with hate and dance with love.

As each song unfolds
These lines of bodies are lost in tones.
Your flesh and your gender all become notes.

So let's roar with the stamping of our feet,
Make earthquakes to rattle the gates of power,
Tear down citadels with this upbeat beat.

We tap messages, our toes are war drums,
Our arms are flailing and scraping the ceiling.
There's a battle plan behind this wiggling bum.

Wake up the neighbours, wake up the nation.
If I can't skank, it's not my revolution.

Each shape we throw is like a battle stance.
It's the Revolution Rumba, the Comrade Conga.
Never mind the Safety Dance; this is the subversive dance.

All those books sit unopened; it's the music which inspires.
It's the Strike Samba and Solidarity Shuffle.
Like the raising of a banner, we turn the volume higher.

Every tiny pinprick of power sung on those songs seeps into
    our heads
And when the final track ends and we slump, victorious, on the
    bed,

We have said all that needs to be said
And stamped as much as needed to be danced.
The foundations have been rattled
And any bug in the room has heard our chorus chants.

We closed the curtains through fear; now they are open wide
And pour morning light inside.
We embrace each other and embrace silences as mere pauses
Between action and action.

In the silence we have created, tired but smiling,
The pride in our noise subsides; we become private.

There are secrets hidden inside the CD cases.
Listen closely to the silences between tracks.
That is the sound of lovers and friends facing
Each other, then the world, and then dancing.

RISE LIKE LIONS (SNAP LIKE TURTLES)

Upstairs, the windows are rattling and the walls brace themselves for impact. He's sitting shaking inside his blankets, poised on his bed. There's a battle inside his head pressing forward and forward against his skull as the weight of armies crushes the fallen at their heels.

He doesn't want to learn something, he wants to hurt something, anger levels rising from *annoyed* to *search and destroy*. Something needs breaking; whether that's a point or a bone, he wants to hear a snap. Feels like the answer to a question he doesn't dare ask.

Feels like he might beat some peace into himself, find relief by mounting war on top of war.

But he grips his pen tight. Decides to put pen to paper and detours the battle lines down his throat, feels the battalions tramp along his arms and bones until they charge forth from his fingers into his pen. The biro sweeps across the page like punches to palms.

When his pen finally rests, his fingers feel sore, but not because they're loaded fists any more.

I've been having trouble sleeping.
Sticks and stones can break our bones, but words are forged weapons.

Rise like lions! Snap like turtles!

I want you to say words so sturdy they can take my full weight. I want you to craft sentences which coil around my neck and choke away my air until I am bluer than summer skies. I want you to form a paragraph as thick as an oak branch. Then we'll play hangman for real.

Let's make a deal. I'll discard my armour, my helmet and my shield. So arm me by telling me something that would make me want to love another human being. Or tell me something that would make me want to hurt another human being.

Sometimes I want to see red like the world's bleeding. I want to breathe fire and melt stone. I want to chew diamonds and crush cars into cubes. Because I've spent too long punching my own palm.

When we drag our ticking timebomb brains out of our bedrooms and onto the barricades we will stand on the desks of struggling writers and the chairs sat upon by lonely musicians. And we will sing until our throats are raw like the eyes of insomniacs.

Because if I listen to music or write or read just before I go to bed, sometimes those words get really deep into my head; I can't get to sleep.

Sticks and stones can break our bones, but words will inspire us.

Rise like lions! Snap like turtles!

REMEMBER WHEN IT RAINED?

Written after the 2015 York floods.

Like someone wasn't just performing a rain dance, but a rain blitz.
   The clouds hadn't burst; they had exploded.
   You'd better bet it got wet as York Minster housed a whale.
   Like a scene from *Shark Tale*, or *Finding Nemo* (which is infinitely better). I kept expecting the Little Mermaid to swim past and complain about the weather.
   I witnessed Poseidon afloat in a raincoat, hoodlum lobsters congregating in parks, sharks out for blood.
   Mercy was reserved for the whims of the Rowing Club.
   The Theatre Royal missed a trick by not staging *Moby Dick* and, what's more, I knew it was bad when SpongeBob SquarePants moved in next door.
   Like when you need the toilet, so there's a downpour in your dreaming.
   This was advanced *Singing in the Rain*. This was torrential screaming.
   Basically, I'm trying to say it was way beyond soggy. Cats and dogs? More like a multitude of mutts and moggies.
   Gone were the days of the dour Yorkshireman stood outside his home, *Racing Post* in one hand, his other catching droplets, who mutters to his whippet, 'It's trying to rain.'
   Well, it wasn't just trying; it was tidal.
   Some indicated climate change, but the fellow in a suit, you know the one, was on telly in underused wellies saying it's nothing to do with that before returning to his second, luxury, insured flat.
   The members of a certain political party pointed their privileged fingers squarely at the Gays, who promptly pointed right back and drowned the bigots beneath the waves.
   At the Travellers' site, no council worker nor police officer appeared, no help nor warning was given
   When someone, somewhere, made that fateful decision
   To raise the Foss Barrier, because it was overworked and failing.
   So I guess someone, somewhere, decided some people's

homes and possessions weren't worth saving.

Across the city, hands got busy, hefting sandbags, typing advice and reports, helping evacuation or simply being at action stations. York neighbours became aware of their neighbourhood despite, or maybe because of, this flooding danger.

You can call this Blitz spirit, or Yorkshire grit, or proof people support each other when put to the test. You can call it a sign of a defiant nation. I think this was just humans in communication.

'Stop sending cash abroad, no more foreign aid,' a few cried as if helping each other is a competition when people suffer, or die.

Imagine a river made of money like a plump, crisp green snake beast. Imagine it becomes a trickle, then a dribble, then its waters cease. Don't blame the hands that dip in for a sip. It's because someone, somewhere, built a dam and the river ran low. Someone redirected what little remained to somewhere more deserving of the flow.

The resources of the world are measured out, mediated and managed and, anything that's in short supply, you can bet your last penny it's the someones somewhere who have most of it.

So sod it! In the morning we said, 'Let's become pirates!'

We hoisted a black flag high and under this exhausted sky roamed the water roads on a ship built from tree branches, wardrobes and spare tyres looted from stranded car boots.

We were a crew made up from the survey suburbs of York, the washouts and the rained. We were the dangerous and unstoppable.

We were like the cast of *Waterworld*, but infinitely more watchable.

Finally, from the crow's nest came a cry: the PM was espied pigging out at a press conference, silky shoulders hefting the weight of 1,001 identical soundbites.

So we made him walk the plank. He spluttered before he stepped. I'll leave you to imagine whether he was mutilated by sharks or just got embarrassingly wet.

Cannons blasted holes in banks with hastily prepared gunpowder

And then we marooned the bankers, top of Clifford's Tower.
   When it's too late to stop the flood, better invest in flotation devices.
   Nothing reveals the importance of resource redistribution like a crisis.
   On new waterways, with expectant eyes to the skies,
   We left York the same way the Vikings arrived.

MY CITY

When my city was young, and still growing up, my city was the kid in the corner of the playground who never looked up. My city was like the kid who spent his days reading and writing, nothing particularly exciting, face down in a history book. My city was taught its identity through a long-dead history.

My city did not play out, could not ride a bike and couldn't play sports to save its life.

When it hit puberty, it was bad with the ladies, didn't quite get the hang of flirting and dating, seemed to spend all its time sat waiting. My city was the kid who looked older than he was.

My city followed all the rules because my city wanted to be a good city, a clean city, present a friendly image. My city became a city that people like to visit.

No matter what my city puts on its list, it always gets aftershave for Christmas. It's that kind of city.

Sometimes, my city talks about your city behind your city's back. Sometimes my city thinks it's better than your city. That's nothing personal to your city; it's just my city is the kind of city your city would want to be. My city got told it was a capital city and my city knows it's talented. My city can come across as kinda arrogant. My city is more of a largish town.

We can get nasty, if we want to. We can spit and rave and rant like the best of them, we can draw great letters of spite and we know how to keep bitterness brewing over long periods of time silently like the rustle of leaves, or crumpled-up paper, or closed parks at night.

We get angry. We get angry like a kid who's scared of monsters, afraid vampires are peckish so he doesn't like to stick his neck out of the covers, I mean, what's that all about?

My city gets nervous and itchy. My city's first thought is often how to lose instead of how to win. My city apologises for things it doesn't lack. My city finds it difficult to make eye contact.

My city might be happy if it stayed at home tonight. My city might leave without saying goodbye and walk home in the rain because that's easier than keeping up a friendly charade. Your city can probably stay up until all hours and coast into the morning like the sunrise over your tower blocks is a collective yawning. I'm sorry, but my city is not like that; my city has last buses to catch.

Take a walk in my city.

When the sun shines, you'll always find a space patch of grass, see old bricks cascade in light and with the sound of a busker in the background things can just feel right. Nestled and secure, my city was a city of safe swords and soldiers. It is protected, its thick walls a humbling shell. It doesn't reach too high, just enough to fit into a tourist's snapshot while the roots sap deep on history. We have maps on display; we pretend not to have mysteries.

My city has a lot of growing up to do.

But my city might just surprise you, because my city surprises me.

My city is the kind of city people like to visit, so sit down and listen.

We cannot teach you about the weaves of the world. Textures of the universe, or cultures we have never met.

Any city can teach you how to hate, and any city can teach you how to love. We will teach you about shortcuts.

We will teach you how to find something you thought we lacked, because we stack company in barrels, put friendship on tap and fill up the glass. Even though, at first glance, we look slow, we're always ready to burst at the banks and overflow.

We will teach you how to sit in a warm room, brightly coloured and surrounded in smells of ales and chocolates, like you're a guest to the aroma. We get warmer as we huddle up close around sofas and tables, find whatever space is available and listen attentively when we're sharing, because we share quietly in this city; we are discreet and polite in the same way cakes sit neatly alongside hot chocolate.

We are a generous city, we are a busy city. If you choose, your calendar can be as full as the rising river in rain, or you can leave this city with disdain. There is more to the city than there appears on billboards and flyers. Reject the middle ground, look up and aim higher.

If you build it, they will come and dance. If you build it, they will come and read. If you build it, they will come to need it.

I have a dream that one day, people of the world will no longer begin every song or project or day with an apology.

Assume apologies are gold. I will buy them a pot of confidence. Pure pints poured on tap with the Mass Text Out taste. The nectar of the faithless.

If a musician makes a sound, they go heard. Typically, that might only be by their own ears. Small rooms and even smaller crowds. My city is awkward silences and apologetic event staff. Sports or arts, we swim in small pools, we are big fish but never sharks. My city is blink-and-you'll-miss-them small business closures; when it's gone, it's missed. My city is feeling depressed about feeling depressed. My city is spontaneous with tears dismissed as temporary floods. Nuisance floods.

But my city is beautiful in the sunshine, or the snow. I hope you know my city is the type of city people like to visit.

We need confidence. We need confidence like... whatever I said, it's what I meant. Let's be our own confidence. In an ideal world, no one would go starving, we graze on our own harvest. We care about each other like we care about air. We need each other, we need our presence and enjoy it so much the angels look down with jealousy, because all the boring people are in heaven. All cities create lives lived in limbo, so if sometimes my city has to be a hell I'll be stoking the fires.

My city's getting there. My city is the kind of city people like to visit. But they don't tend to stay. They move away.

We've been walking for a while, so just find a comfortable corner and settle down. Cosy seats and friendly off-and-on mates. Passive-aggressive undertones to keep us awake. Then tell me about your city.

TOBY THE TYRANNOSAURUS REX

Most people's pets are alright, I suppose.
Pretty standard as far as pets go.
But in our house, we have a guest
Called Toby, and he's a Tyrannosaurus rex.

He's my best friend, he's got scales and sharp claws.
Instead of talking, he just bellows and roars.
Some say he's a Jurassic threat,
Toby the Tyrannosaurus rex.

You'll find him in the teapot, down your trouser leg or on top of the telly.
We lost Toby once but he'd just gone to sleep in my welly.
If you meet Toby, you might be a little bit perplexed
Because Toby is a tiny Tyrannosaurus rex.

You'll find him driving toy trucks, toy trains and toy tractors.
He's the little king of the dinosaurs, not some wimpy raptor.
He's so little you might need to put on your specs
To catch a glimpse of Toby the tiny Tyrannosaurus rex.

But what he lacks in size, Toby makes up for in guts.
He's not afraid of anything, he's brave and he's tough.
If you outstay your welcome, he'll go for your legs.
He's Toby the tiny, terrible Tyrannosaurus rex.

All up my street, they whisper to one another,
'If you see the prehistoric monster, run for cover.'
They get nervous, they shake, they break out in a sweat.
Beware of Toby the tiny, terrible Tyrannosaurus rex.

They said, 'We've come to lodge a list of complaints.'
They said, 'You've got to do something about your little mate.'
They said, 'I'm afraid all us neighbours are scared and upset
About your tiny, terrible, untameable Tyrannosaurus rex.'

I said, 'Yeah, he may be vicious,

And yeah, he may be dangerous,
But what did you expect?
He's Toby the tiny, terrible, untameable Tyrannosaurus rex.'

You see, Toby is loyal to his closest friends.
He'll defend me until the very end.
With a friend like Toby, I've got no regrets,
Because my best friend is a tiny, terrible, untameable,
    tenacious Tyrannosaurus rex.

He's always got my back; when I'm asleep, he stands guard.
Some people have teddy bears; I've got a tyrant lizard.
So show some respect
To Toby the tiny, terrible, untameable, tenacious Tyrannosaurus
    rex.

UP THE NERD PUNKS 2

Just when you thought punk was dead like Ned (Stark),
'Up the Nerd Punks' is back!
It's back like the films of the eighties.
It's back like *Robot Wars*,
Back like *Samurai Jack*.
It's back like Ryan Reynolds' career.
It's back like an evil female Tory prime minister.
'Up the Nerd Punks' will return like a rebrandable spy.
It's the *Return of the King*, *Return to Oz* and *Return of the Jedi*.
Return to the Forbidden Planet (to buy more comics).
Difficult second albums are a myth; this show wasn't hard.
Look at *Doolittle*, *Nevermind* and *Blisters in the Pit of My Heart*.
Sometimes it's right the sequel is better than the first.
It's Skanking Spider-Man 2, the Dork Knight, it's the Wrath of
    Tim Kharmstrong.
It's the storm after the calm,
It's the bite after a bark,
The boom after the click,
The crash after the throw,
Plus all my merchandise has to go.
The nerd punks are back,
Flying in using a Littlefinger jetpack
Or a Varys speedboat.
I'm back, scrawny but still angry,
Buzzing with nerd punk energy.
Pleased to meet you, Henry Raby.
It's 2016. There's a new Blink-182 album, and everyone's
    playing Pokémon Go.
It's like we've gone back in time.
What is this, 1999?

PokéRap Round Two,
Generation Two,
I'm taking you on like it's 2001.
Whether it's morning, day or night,
No matter the time, prepare to fight,
'Cause now when I'm fighting I'm holding onto items.

Can't beat me now; I'm made of steel.
Cracking open eggs for my next meal,
I hatch and see you're a Togepi.
Last thing I need is to eat berries with a baby.
Rollout, Bounce, just Hoppip, I'm a Hitmontop with a Triple Kick.
Like a nightmare-chewing Misdreavus my pain is grievous.
You're in trouble, I'm a Shuckle and my Defence is double.
Like the bite of a Granbull, this pain is inevitable.
Ho-Oh! Trying to Sneasel your way out of this.
Listen, little Teddiursa, I don't want to have to hurt ya,
But I'll give you a Skarmory; nowhere's too far for me.
I just hop on the Magnet Train.
What will be will be. Celebi.

I'll be looking through my Pokédex to capture your cries
Until it's several years later and my clock battery has died.

What's changed in the last few years?
Star Wars came back, and people got mad
Because it boasted a diverse cast.
Harry Potter came back, and people got mad
Because it boasted a diverse cast.
Ghostbusters came back, and people got mad
Because it boasted a diverse cast.
So draw swords, clash of chords,
The nerd punks are going to war!

FIVE CANS OF DEODORANT

Becoming a man means you have to make some difficult decisions. Here's one of them. I could get up this morning. Or I could stay in bed that little while longer before school. Rest my head on this plump pillow, sink back into dreams and wrap up tight in this duvet. I poke a toe outside the sheets, test the atmosphere. The toe zips back like a retreating scout into the warm embrace of the bed.

I leave it till the very last possible second, and on the final tick I arise from my bed like a shuffling zombie, my eye firmly on the clock and finger firmly on the snooze button. I get ready for school in a hurry, dealing with priority tasks like toast and internet over homework, books and a shower.

Cut to later in the day. At school I feel like I'm being watched. Everyone else's eyes follow me down the corridor, stare at me in the classroom, record me in the playground. I feel like I'm being stalked by the entire school population, and behind my back I'm the number one topic of conversation.

Everything everyone notices about me is bad. My hair is far from stylish; it's a messy bush. I've not washed my face properly, so it's a rough surface of pimples and spots. I didn't bother getting a paper round, so I can't afford the best shoes, and I never bother to exercise, so I must be fat and huge.

I get picked out by being so normal. I feel like a stock character in a film who doesn't have any lines, but the camera stalks them and never leaves their side. I feel like the only one at a costume party not wearing a disguise, like the runner-up in the competition unfairly walking away with the prize.

There's lads who are allowed to stay out late at night, lads who reckon they can win any fight. Boys who get all the best grades and praise, and when something bad happens there's boys who smile and shrug when they take all the blame. I'm not bad at football, but I'm not the best; I'm not bad in lessons but I don't pass every test. I'm just the character without a story. There's lads who know everything there is to know about girls, drink and even drugs. But I bet I know the most about love.

There's a girl. Alright, cliché, I know, there's always a girl. But she's *the* girl. If I had to be a hero, I would choose to save her before the world. That would make me a real main character.

I can see her in my dreams. I dream about her being my girlfriend, I dream about her being the mother to my children. I dream about us cuddling in bed.

But the problem is, I'm a problem. She's as interested in me as an OAP is keen on riding the dodgems, she cares about me like a lion cares about using doors. If she had to choose, I bet she'd rather chat to a brick wall.

In geography, I keep making excuses to go to the bin to sharpen my pencil. I'm not regretful; I'd rather hover near her than draw an oxbow lake. I sharpen slowly, stand at just the right angle, and listen closely. She and her friends make plans, meeting in the local park by streetlight with intentions for a great night.

My stealth is unveiled; I've dawdled too long. They make a handful of comments, and my whole body goes rigid, my mouth dry like a desert, and my heart starts hurting. I turn to them, pause (for dramatic effect) and then ask if it would be alright if I came along. Tonight. Maybe. Possibly. Please.

That night I'm trying hard to remain calm, trying hard not to start walking on the ceiling, trying hard to slow down... and then trying hard not to try so hard. I scour through my clothes, choosing exactly the right top, trousers, socks, underpants and even handkerchief. I try a million different styles on my hair and breeze through a lifetime's supply of gel. I scrub my face so it's less spotty (but slightly raw and hurty). I even have a shave. A slight shave of a handful of hairs, I admit, but the buzzer feels like a weapon in my grip.

Her words swim around my head, committed to memory and part of my manifesto for tonight. Make sure you use some deodorant. *Make sure you use some deodorant. Make sure you use some deodorant. Make sure you use some deodorant.*

I make sure I use some deodorant.

I spray and spray. I put the can down. What if I still stink? I select another can. I spray and spray. But, just to be on the safe side, I find my dad's deodorant and make sure my left armpit is fully insured. Then I find my brother's and make sure my right armpit is fully insured. My eyes go sore, I fumble for the bedroom door. The room is a haze of mist, but maybe, I think, it could seal a kiss.

I take a glance at my toys piled in the corner of my room, and I scoff as I, a grown man, leave the house with the taste of victory (and, I hope, smelling satisfactory).

On the way I stop off at the local supermarket and buy another can of spray. Just to be on the safe side.

I arrive in good time, act cool, hang around, hands in pockets. Chat to a few people at the meeting spot. Then she arrives. I sidle up to the girl, give a friendly smile. She's going to say something. I can see my life unfolding before me, us holding hands, kissing, getting engaged, marrying, children, grandchildren, growing old together and finally, holding hands tightly, embracing, we gently pass away.

She looks at me with disapproval. Her eyes turn to a glare. She opens her mouth to say, 'You stink of spray!'

KINGDOMS

My bedroom is my kingdom.

I refuse to comb my hair; it forms a messy duck's-bottom crown, evidence of a decent night's sleep of dreams. The window has been left open and now birds tweet off in the distance and cars form the soundtrack to a warm morning. A Saturday morning. A no-school day. And today my kingdom has guests, foreign ambassadors here on an official visit, dignitaries of another far-off kingdom. My bedroom is my kingdom.

They enter into my kingdom, a world where the tapestry of wallpaper is disguised by a secondary wall of posters sealed with stale Blu-Tack. Photographs adorn select spots; postcards, paintings and other pictures serve as a sliding scale of memory. I also keep a tick on the wall as my height grows. I am learning what nostalgia means.

There's Board Game Mountain in the corner, a collection of worlds squished into two dimensions; instruction manuals form the law of these worlds.

My visitors and I cheerfully battle, sharing our swords which comprise joysticks, buttons and leads attached to merrily humming boxes. I am not the best combatant in this arena; my scores pale at times. Though I am getting better.

I entreat my visitors to meet the denizens of my kingdom, toys and plastic men and women who live packed inside inhospitable boxes, loosed upon the sprawling floor.

But those boxes are opened less and less, until finally the dust upon them is embarrassingly thick.

My house is my kingdom.

My kingdom has been invaded. But it's my party, which still makes me the king. Admittedly a king who has trouble standing up. My subjects are in rebellion, fuelled by cheap booze and an assortment of tunes, varying from the disturbingly addictive pop to some skankable ska.

This is my first foray into the Age of Alcohol. As a forest of cans, bottles and wine glasses grows ever thicker in swathes and clusters, we the valiant warriors attempt to quell this spread with all the courage and vigour we can muster.

We are no longer in training. The hours roll into night and those committed to remaining have marked their spots. Hidden their secret stashes, informed parents, deliberately missed buses and cancelled taxis. The practice is over. The party has made us bolder, and, accompanied with the roar of peer pressure, the notion of a single session has evolved into a mead-hall-style dare war.

Things are thrown, things are drunk, things are eaten. Mighty deeds are undertaken which will enter the annals of legend.

Someone pulls out an acoustic guitar.

I'm not a gambling man, but bets can be placed on who-gets-with-who, a traditional dance which combines the best elements of naïve optimism and base sleaze. Corners, sleeping bags, spare rooms, bathrooms and even cupboards become romantic locations, predictable sites only hazily remembered but never forgotten.

The party seeps outside under a cloud of smoke and smiles. Those still with a sense of navigation escape to the open air to disgustingly allow their stomachs that little extra space. I am far too gone to contemplate such sensible matters, and disturb an unlucky couple who wish they'd chosen a more secure location.

The morning can be described in one word: painful. If all one's aims have been fulfilled, the mouth will be dry and the head will be dull. If the night is the Valhalla, I have entered the bacon-butty-fuelled when-will-this-queasy-feeling-stop Ragnarok.

My city is my kingdom.

I have sworn myself to predictability. I feel like this town has taught me everything I need to know and to stay here would be a case of routine nine-to-five-style Stockholm syndrome.

But don't get me wrong; this tradition isn't undesirable. Old habits die hard and I won't dare tame that old wild animal. But these are the same old dances with the same partners I know. I haven't got sick of the song, but I learnt all the words a long time ago. And there are new worlds to conquer, new streets to wander down and challenges you just can't undertake in my hometown.

The bags are packed. I'll start this new course, I'll pay those fees and, hopefully, get into a bit of mischief at this predictable university. It's nothing new these days, they say; degrees mean less and less. It's a cliché, but as long as I'm happy now, I know an old man who would have been proud.

My town intends to give me a decent send-off, so who knows where I'll end up? My loan's just come in, so I'll probably be spent up. But before that, it takes half the night debating on our target location and preference of pub. There have been political manifestos that took less time to draw up than choosing where to drink, getting up and go.

But for tonight we are the kings of this town, we've got an endless supply of red paint and we make sinners out of saints. We hit pubs like battering rams, we put more booze inside us than is behind the bar, if the road home is too long then we'll simply sleep out under the stars. We sing old traditional songs our fathers and mothers sang. Stuff like the Pogues and the Jam.

I can't wait to be the new king of my new city.

LOST

You know when you've lost something, and you just can't find it?
And that little thing you've lost is the most important item in the world.
So you look in the cupboard, under floorboards,
Behind the sofa, in the wardrobe,
And that little thing you've lost is the most important thing in the world, because you decided it.
Sometimes the thing you've lost is a memory you swear was there before.
You take out your private set of keys, try and unlock every door.
But memories aren't always where you thought they were before.
There's no last place to look because there's no first place to explore.
And it's a long way to the dawn, and you think you've had enough.
And what you're really looking for is some strength and love.
But that's not in some cartoon or some stupid kids' comic.
And it's a long way to the dawn, and you've had enough.
And what you're really looking for is some strength and love.
But that's not in some play or stupid old song.
And it's a long way to the dawn, and you know you've had enough.
And you're wondering if what will remain of you will even remotely resemble love.
Do you remember standing beside that great wide bed, the bed that drowned an immortal?
Do you remember your disappointment as they lay weak and humourless?
Do you remember the hushed conversations with the experts, the way you strained to hear calculated apologies?
Do you remember the silences, the respect you lost witnessing awkwardness amongst adults?
Do you remember closing your eyes and re-opening them into an older world of tears and serious faces?
Do you remember trying desperately to tally their loves, their memories, their stories and their healthier face?

And do you remember feeling ashamed you thought their
    words would be lost?
And do you remember you made them smile by unlocking a
    simple, small memory?
How could I forget?

ECHO CHAMBER (FAR AWAY IN TIME)

Join me inside my echo echo echo chamber
Where polls are passed around like a pat on the back.
Where debates end before they begin with a quick 'I know, right?'
Likes and RTs keep me warm all through the night
Even though it's too dark outside to see.
I know, somewhere in the world,
Someone agrees with me.
I offer my opinion, and with a beautiful bounce it comes back home.
Repetition helps cement something I already know.

Friends, please remember, this is nothing new.
Once we worked within our class.
We drank from pint glasses or goblets.
We ate from lunch boxes or in feast halls.
We built castles, or we sat upon thrones within them.
'What do you think of this king fellow, then?'
'He's alright, but it's pretty naff being a peasant.
Mud. Famine. And when he calls to war we get hurt.'
Thus appeareth a sheriff, flanked by knights, who sayeth:
'Traitors! Scoundrels! Villainy! Thou forget'st thy function.
Get thee into the Echo Dungeons.'
I guess tribalism never really died
When one community gets funding, and the other fed lies.

NERD PUNKS 3D

Comics, cartoons, board games, fantasy and sci-fi,
Politics, protest, subversion and DIY.
Plonk us in fictional settings and we'll ignore all orders.
We're gonna put on our headphones and damn well walk into Mordor.
We're quite selective when it comes to following the Prime Directive.
It's dangerous to go alone? Well, we'll rock up as a collective.
Joining a union puts a different meaning to 'boss battle'.
If the NHS gives us health points, the Tories are mid-game execution.
Good thing in choosing a general election they hurt themselves in their confusion.
Whoever sits on the Iron Throne, Lannister, Snow or Dragon Queen,
We still know you ain't no human being.
Where we're going, we don't need bros.
The internet is a nasty place. Trolls in the dungeons of the web.
It's hard to 'just get over being offended' when someone wants you dead.
The alt-right make memes, pretend they find faith in an Egyptian deity.
They say they want free speech but take away human liberties.
No one says the Death Eaters have genuine concerns or policies.
No; they are magical Nazis.
And when it comes to race, if one side is screeching
'EXTERMINATE'
That's a fight we need to face.
You've got to ask 'which side am I on?' sooner or later.
Probably not the one that would appeal to Darth Vader.

We're the non-playable characters, the knock-off controller.
We're the cheat code broken, ripped-up scroll, glitching side-scroller.
We're the level one cannon fodder gone wrong.
Fuck you; I'm going to carry seven Pokémon.

But I stopped playing the game in 2001.
If spoken word means honesty,
No one really loves Pokémon's Generation III.
I'm sorry to Ruby salt in your wound,
Incur your Sapphire,
Sorry to knock Pokéblocks
But I ain't goin' to Hoenn.

So now the box office is boxing nerd culture for the masses.
There's never been a wider gap between the rich and the working classes.
Each day the Dark Lords push us closer to the end of the world
And people start to panic when *Doctor Who* tries to appeal to girls.
So are we winning by raising the flag for diversity?
Or are they still turning rebellion into money?
This is a commercial for how the world got commercial.
Did Ned Stark die just so you could gorge on merchandise?
Do you really need a *Rick and Morty* lampshade in your life?
Meanwhile the following things are rising:
Sea levels.
Temperatures.
Corporate power.
Fascism.

So, friends, let's save the world.
So, Doc, let's go back to the past,
Flux capacitor and eighty-eight miles an hour.
Stereo blasting a playlist is the real power.
Squat the TARDIS, it's pretty roomy.
Hijack and fly it through all of history.
I'm a good student, hand me a Time-Turner.
I'll be back to pick up a time displacement sphere.
Rend asunder the lesson from *Sound of Thunder*.
Wormholes, time portals and magic spells,
Blinding light, days of future past.
HG Wells made me a believer.

Playing rock and roll on the Ocarina.
Replay my favourite bands because I'm a Looper.
Let's play make-believe like we used ta.

ONE HUNDRED YEARS

1917, her hands cradle a plump handful of ticklish white feathers. She has been ordered to distribute them to the conscientious objectors. She's told: 'This is how we will be gifted the vote.' But encouraging men to kill other men isn't how she wants to use her citizenship. If fighting for the vote means fighting a fellow human, she raises the peace banner ever higher and realises this fight is much harder.

1939, his hands hold the newspapers. Reads about the fascist flags in Madrid, Berlin and Rome. The same flags waved by British Blackshirts in British streets. The same flags *hurrah*ed by the *Daily Mail*. Six years later he sits in sweat, a twitch in his palm that does not trust the recent amnesty. To make this war worth it, he uses his trembling hand to place an X by the party promising to build a National Health Service.

1968, her hands feel the grooves of the neat black vinyl bought from Woolworths with precious pennies. It spins a friendly tune of distant Jamaica, a gift to her boyfriend to remind him of a slice of another life. He arrives with a bloody face, his thick black wiry hair matted with red, a parting gift from loyal men quoting a racist politician whose self-fulfilling prophecy predicts rivers of blood. They both know there's going to be some rage to go with their love.

1990, her hand grips the placard stick like a lifeline in the middle of London. Noise comes in battalions, coppers come in ranks. Into the melee she recruits a cry of 'No poll tax'. Breath is minimised, stomach is tense, this is the climax of a long hard decade of greed. The officer doesn't say a word; he just sweeps his baton like a breeze and she screams, but refuses to drop to her knees.

2010, the doors are locked with thick bike locks, the banner above is still damp with paint, reads: *OCCUPY*. They tap Tweets across the globe, this lecture theatre becomes a second home. Community is localised, community is global, this method is young, this fight is old. They know education should not be bought and sold.

Because their mother has a scar from Trafalgar Square, their grandfather was missing an ear and their great-grandfather couldn't hold a pen. Their ancestor was tortured by the state whilst fighting for woman's rights. So they'll be damned if they're being evicted from this place tonight. They meet the police officer's gaze.

'You lot just want the world on a plate,' the officer says. They reply: 'We're far more ambitious than that.'

VISION OF UTOPIA

The present is a white-hot battlefield stinking of cannon fire.
Through bitter eyes stinging in the smoke
We see a vision of a future in bloom:
A red carnation.
Louise Michel is born today in France, 1830.
Teacher, poet, revolutionary,
A lover of writing, and science.
Weapons are both pens and rifles.
For her, fairgrounds were target practice.
Education is a revolutionary tactic.
Today, March 1871, starved by a war with Prussia,
The people of Paris refuse to accept authority of the French government.
When sent to enforce state power, the National Guard refuse to shoot
Their own people dead.
Today, April 1871 in Paris, they sing a red song.
As the streets bellow opera,
The factories whistle their own tune.
This is the new Paris Commune.
A red-hot spark of working-class control,
Co-operation, redistribution,
Social justice, education.
And Louise, like thousands of women,
Roots herself into the struggle.

This week, May 1871, is a bloody week.
The French Army spills red revolutionary blood in the street.
The dissident Communards dig their own graves.
The neighbours complain about the shots,
So the condemned are bayoneted to death.
Louise is exiled to New Caledonia,
Pacific island in the blue of France's empire.
Louise sees the power of white colonial control.
She befriends, defends and shows solidarity.
Today, 1873, she fights not for the rights
But the very existence of native people
Against state control.

Today, 1880, upon her return to France she still hasn't learnt
To obey,
Neither the state that imprisons her body
Nor the liberals who lack a bright red bold vision.

The National Guard did not fire at Louise, at their own people.
They made their stand, so this is Louise's lesson.
Today, in schools, in work, in the red mist,
Make a fist and see the vision of utopia.
North Yorkshire Police. The Metropolitan Police. The UK
 Border Patrol. The ATOS assessor.
The ones who burn the Calais Jungle, the ones who plunge us
 deeper.
It's simple: do not fire on the people.
Just me, and Louise, and you
On the barricades tomorrow, together
In this red vision of utopia.

MY IMPOSTER

I may not know much about interdimensional travel,
But the rift between dimensions must be thinner than a hungry Monday morning,
Cupboards unstacked and chores unattacked,
Weak like lacking strength to see the appropriate adult side of 10am.
The wall between dimensional spaces is fragile like own-brand tissues,
Because I have seen my Imposter.
A proper doppelganger from another world has made his way to York.
I've seen him in Parliament Street, in Foxwood, along Lord Mayor's Walk.
Doesn't even have the gall to grow a whip-thin moustache, wear a top hat and tie damsels to train tracks.
My Imposter is trying to infiltrate my life one event at a time, pleased to play the part of the invited guest.
Friends can't tell the difference; he's me made of other atoms.
We are a pair of band-T-shirt-wearing mirrored patterns
I first suspected his infiltration at a celebration.
A party with an atmosphere humming Sunday summer warmth and stretching smiles across a riverbank
Got the barbecue and made people laugh.
Got the beers out and held eye contact.
Instantly the sort of fellow you'd like to befriend.
Eventually left, but only when the party came to its end.
He must come from a much more confident dimension, where casualness comes quicker than claustrophobia.
Since then I have seen my Imposter at parties, social gatherings, events and the theatre. It was actually him at that gig, rehearsal and poetry recital.
I have seen my Imposter down the pub get the round in, get you a double, pay for the taxi and do everything perfectly.
I have seen my Imposter raise toasts and even dare to boast, load up cupboards with food, arrive on time and smile at your jokes.
I have seen my Imposter pay the bills and do the taxes and

do the gardening and reply to emails and catch up with
my grandparents.
I'd like to tell you, honestly, that's not me, that's my evil twin
who got into this world and can't get out.
I'd like to tell you, honestly, that's not me, that's my evil fraud
full of phoney unHenryness you keep seeing around.
I'd like to tell you, but I'm afraid if my cruel suspicions were
known, he'd flee, and I feel sorry for him because he can't
get back home.

POST-APOCALYPSE ADVISORY

What happens when the world ends? What happens to the words?
When civilisation grinds to a halt, while we sit upon irradiated dirt,
Will we still take pen to precious paper and use it to write verse?
Apocalyptic poetry for apocalyptic times!
It's the end of the world as we know it, and I feel the need to rhyme!
Who knows, maybe that comet will just fly on by.
In the zombie apocalypse, the main theme of poetry will be brains.
This will raise rotten results, shuffling and sluggish wordplay.
'BRAINS BRAINS BRAINS. Brains! Brains, brains. Brains? *Brains.*'
(And some acts will still read from the page.)

Water, water everywhere and not a drop to drink.
Let's write some poems to keep afloat hopes before they sink.
It seems the film *Waterworld* might be more realistic than we think.

Unfortunately there won't be flowers. Or bees.
Please welcome famine, war, death and disease,
A killer poetry collective slam team.

I wandered lonely as a radioactive cloud.
I have eaten the plums that were in the ice box, before the tentacle monsters got there first.
They fuck you up, your mum and dad. And then they eat you.

Punk poetry. Found poetry. Freestyle poetry.
These all lack teeth and guts. Specifically, razor-sharp teeth and guts full of bubbling acids. Let's really chew on the substance of the piece, let's tear into the content, let's rip the poet to bits.
Add mutant poetry to your reading lists.

Shhhh. Don't scribble so loudly; the alien conquerors might hear you.

Welcome to the Thunderdome, where gladiatorial combat pits slam poet against slam poet,
Each covered in spikes, studs and an awkward abundance of leather.
WHAT A DAY, WHAT A LOVELY DAY to sit and read some poetry…
Where, without a structure, we find faith in the structure of verse and we can aspire…
Oh, shit, forget all that bollocks, someone's just gone and re-invented fire.

We hold each other as the spaceship, housing all humanity's hopes, becomes a speck in the sky.
Well, most of humanity's hopes.
It leaves behind a handful of us stood, with eager hands
Making new, less shiny and space-age plans.
Just you, me and the cockroaches
Sharing poetry.

I suppose when the tectonic plates break,
World-changing poetry will feel forced and fake.
In the face of landmass-scale catastrophe, how can we articulate?
The broken world must home broken words.
As we rebuild our fragile rock in the universe,
What have we learnt?
If we have seen the vastness be shattered, we must value the tiny things.
Fresh water.
Dog licks.
Rare grins.
Words failed us; we could not avert this end of the world.
But I'd like to think, against the sounds of Armageddon, poetry could still be heard.
I'd like to think there'd still be worth in words on lips post-apocalypse.

TV ON DEMAND

Home is where the heart knows it can't escape.
It charges itself, time and time again, against the bone gates.
It is your private army, built for battle,
Whether or not you are winning the war.
My house was a ship, the landing the deck.
You'd better bet I was a pirate and the street the ocean,
Dad the merchant ship targeted to receive cannon explosions.
I got a parrot, a cutlass, wooden leg, hook for a hand…
It took me until I was twenty-seven to actually read *Treasure Island*,
Around the time me and Dad sat down to watch season four of *Game of Thrones*.
In an attempt to save money, we'd taped it off Sky Atlantic,
But the Sky+ shuddered and stuttered
And no one wants to see a Red Viper disjointed.
The image skips like a heartbeat bolting from its box,
A scuffed memory escaping off into the middle distance.
One of us said, 'Never mind,' but sentences didn't synch up to lips.
The shrug is a pulse of nerves going unnoticed.
Some words are lost.
Upstairs was a box of Bonds, the kind that kill then quip,
Aardman and Asterix and every version of *Treasure Island* you can imagine
Tied tight inside black VHS.
Memory wears your old band T-shirts.
Memory rereads your favourite books.
It listens to your CDs, quotes you, knows you,
But stands off in the distance, at the other end of Hob Moor like the lights of Lidl
Guiding a torchless adventurer through the labyrinth of cowpats.
When Home meets Memory it can be like rewatching your life in a documentary.
The *Star Wars* saga you invented with your figures was just released onto Netflix.
That last ever prayer you said before bed is track three on the

Greatest Hits.
Rewatch the first kiss on channel +1.
A compilation of best gigs ever is on YouTube to view,
And a playlist for the gigs you played too.
Will Henry survive downing that dirty pint? This is the
    cliffhanger to season three.
If you missed you struggling at university, don't worry, it's on
    catch-up TV.
Download the podcast mainly of quotes you can't remember.
Thank the Old God it doesn't stay this way forever.
So, heart, settle down, because you can't escape.
You can beat, skip, shudder and race.
When Memory meets Home, there's nowhere left for the heart
    to go,
So it trembles inside its calcium cage as the life outside plays on.
And that's really TV on demand.

LOVE ME, I'M A MILLENNIAL

The 1980s produced 'Town Called Malice', popularised *Dallas* and brought Diana into the Palace.
They also produced me in 1988, brought up post-Berlin Wall, post-miners' strike, post -New Romantic.
By the time I came of age Thatcherism had a legacy in New Labour's tactics.
Today I stream the 1990s on a machine designed by people born in that decade.
I wear T-shirts depicting cartoons to indicate my age.
My generation's bands are respected, but not as respected as the bands who came before.
I'm connected to the world through my phone, so my hand is like a dragon claw.
I spend a lot of time job hunting and training for non-existent work.
I'm gathering all my friends, and acquaintances (and people I just met once, or have seen around) on social networks.
Do they still use overhead projectors in schools?
No? Oh, well, whatever, never mind; at least my mum says I'm cool.
So love me, love me, love me, I'm a Millennial.

I was told to follow my dreams in this new twenty-first century.
Educational opportunities open a world of possibilities,
A whole new world of working-class social mobility.
I became yet another student who stewed at university.
What do you do with all that learning?
I'll let you know after some unpaid interning.
The rent comes courtesy of a tips jar,
The tips jar is courtesy of the manager,
The manager comes courtesy of the company,
The company sells tips jars commercially,
And that's the backbone of the British economy.
Love me, love me, love me, I'm a Millennial.

I remember *Goosebumps* and *Rugrats* and Cotton-Eye Joe.
When did the '00s become retro?

I casually use words like *problematic* and *call-out*.
My lexicon is littered with LOLs and ROFLs.
I'm indebted to my grandparents for fighting fascism,
I'm indebted to my parents for propping up the welfare state,
I'm in debt...
The first rung of the property ladder collapsed.
I looked up to see the house prices and my neck snapped.
Right to buy? Privatisation? Deregulate the markets?
Slow hand clap.
I totally haven't got a plan.
I'm almost thirty years old.
I'm adulting as hard as I can.
Kids today have it so good.
We used to have to blow on our games to get rid of dust.
My generation felt so progressive in 2010
In voting for the Lib Dems.
I dust off the Nintendo 64
Or put a begging cap on the floor.
Nowadays we call them conflicts, not wars.
So love me, love me, love me, I'm a Millennial.

What do you want as a pet? A unicorn.
What do you want to be when you grow up? A unicorn.
What are you going to name your firstborn? Unicorn Raby.
I want to leap to my generation's defences.
We're more likely to spend our money on experiences.
The generation with the favourite emoji.
The generation that generated the meme.
The generation with Pokémon bedsheets.
Hell yes, we're living the dream.
The generation least likely to vote.
The generation least likely to love a god.
We're just waiting for the baby boomers to die so we can take
    their jobs.
Anxiety? Panic attacks? Self-doubt?
True, you can't simply Google *What's it all about?*
So you grew up in the shadow of nuclear warheads and bombs?

The solution isn't stiff upper lips, keeping calm and carrying on.
Do I feel entitled? No, I'm just owed a fucking living.
You call it a free market economy, I call it a prison.
So love me, love me, love me, I'm a Millennial.

The clue's in the name; imagine in 2000 that we entered a new age.
The internet put music, art, ideas and connectivity in handy webpages
Still felt hate, still felt wars of class and race, still Section 28,
Your parliaments and unions and laws past their best.
We've only just had a chance to get to use the NHS.
We get so politically engaged it makes us stressed,
So we go on Buzzfeed and rank which Disney era was best instead.
When catering for a career or managing a mortgage is immaterial
We may as well just debate our favourite cereals.

Things were so much better in the past, right?
Things will be so much better in the future, right?
Let's watch *Adventure Time* all night.
We'll make the world better, just have some patience.
Too late; we gentrified our generation.
As long as the rising sea levels don't drown 'em,
Place your faith in those born after 2000,
For you see,
Love me, love me, love me, I'm a Millennial.
#TLDR

BRITAIN 3D

The camera pans across the wide forests, seas of green.
Robin Hood pops his head up, hood up, and nicks some sweets.
There's a sword in the stone in the grounds of a stately home.
If you get membership, you can even try and pull it out.
The lads down the street are feeling ever so bold, they rock up, give it a go.
The library explodes, the hospital explodes, the cockney corner caff explodes, Betty's tea room explodes!
Sudden cut to an actor rehearsing his lines at the Globe Theatre before curtain up.
The audience demanded it, so this performance will see real blood.
Richard III, with realistic gore. The audience applaud, they want more.
Meanwhile the lads are still giving it a go at the sword, draped in flags, spitting with sweat, sweating with spit.
There's a group out with placards but they're ignored. Just kids.
There's a red button on a desk in a room with comfy chairs.
There's a boat loaded with cash that's off to visit another shore.
There's a subplot about wealth and where it came from.
It links back to Africa and the Americas, but the film is already overlong.
There's a song, there's a tune, there's a pop single for the radio waves.
There's a singer in a bedroom and she plays guitar night and day.
The lads are still trying to get this sword out, they've had a few cans.
They'd chant their demansds, if they could remember the plan.
On Ceefax it's actually factual to find a piece of art that grabs you.
We're a nation of poets and novelists, so words sell it best.
There's a chap in a suit of armour still looking for a damsel in distress.
There's a historian who wrote the history books in tears, like there's something he needs to get off his chest.

There's smoke, so there's a fire. There's a finger and blame.
There's a council of soundbites all playing the same game.
And in the middle of the cast of millions is me, in Bristol, a good few hours on the train from my home.
I'm standing in front of a giant map of the UK and plotting all the places I've gone.
I'm trying to memorise places I've never been for future reference.
Blurring the lines between Seeing the World and a touring collection.
Places birth people, and people build community.
People also build worlds and put walls around them.
They name them, they fight for them, they live and die there,
And you can see it all if you can afford the rail fare.

THREE MINUTES TO SAVE THE WORLD

Use life straws to purify water.
Smokeless stoves, home birth kits.
Distribute sanitary pads.
Steer clear of nuclear.
Walk, cycle, get on the bus
(When it finally arrives).
Recycle, reuse, reclaim, retake.
Eat less meat. Eat no meat.
Time machines are pretty pricey, but if we all chip in, we can send someone back in time
To 1999, where they can party,
2001, where they can issue a warning,
1933, where they can prepare for things to come.
I guess what's done is done.

Turn. Off. The. Lights.
Get a bike. Stroke dogs. Adopt dogs.
Smile at strangers. Make eye contact.
Turn off your phone. Smash your phone.
Don't look at me. Don't smile if you don't want to.
Worry your parents. Dye your hair bright colours.
Your existence exists.
Think positive thoughts before bed.
Re-listen to 'Tubthumping' to get the blood pumping.
Get knocked down. Get up again.
Defy. Redirect. Resist.
Ban the bomb.
Food, not bombs.
Admit something went wrong.
Admit it couldn't be fixed.
Throw some bricks.
Tax the rich.
Steal from the rich.
Eat the rich.
March. Strike. Occupy.
Say goodnight. Say goodbye.

Plant trees. Find a cure for disease.
Support charities. Support the public sector.
Look at your work. Can it get better?
Rewrite and redraft. Hone your craft.
Go to workshops, go to symposiums.
Free write every day.
There's more than one way.
Don't repeat yourself, don't write the same poem over and over again.
Don't repeat yourself, a full stop doesn't mean you've reached the end.
If you believe you have no confidence: everything you write astounds me.
If you are big-headed, calm down, learn some humility.
Stop egging on egos; confidence conflicts with arrogance.
Find out what you hate and don't become one.
Stare into the abyss.
Give it a gift.
Get to know it.
If it stares into you,
Cook a meal for two.

Learn to change yourself for good.
Donate blood.
Spread love.
Cuddle sloths.
Don't touch me.
Wash your hands.
Gender is fluid and free.
There is no normality to sexuality.
Push idols off pedestals, learn some history.
Decolonise, open a safe space, go be unsafe.
Understand your place in past evil's legacies.
Smoke less, less is more.
Stop the war.
Invest in the youth, invest in science.
I might be biased, but invest in the arts.

Cover your guitar in stickers.
Demand your friends form bands.
Support your local art scene.
Be an audience member.
If it's pay-what-you-can,
Pay a little more when you can.
Learn three chords.
If you can, learn a few more.
Don't write songs about how a girl left you heartbroken.
Boo-hoo. Nobody cares.

If the ship is sinking, don't spend time reshuffling deckchairs.
Don't go down with it, learn to swim.
There is no binary of lose and win.
Build communities.
Form communes.
Vote Labour.
Vote Green.
Vote for me.
Refuse to vote.
Dismantle this illusion of democracy.
Smash this restrictive hierarchy.
Stop the pipelines.
Stop thinking *This is mine.*
Un-name the rivers, the mountains, the seas.
A flag in the ground, a line on a map, a deed to land
Won't make you free.
Open borders, live wherever.
Human race survives together.
Rip up your ticket for the rocket.
Never mind the second Earth, find worth in this dirt.

Understand the difference between what is right
And what they deem a crime.
Rethink how you go about thinking.
Be brave. Be bold. Be another synonym.
Eat healthy. Take showers. Boots are made for walking.

Get off social media. Communicating isn't always verbally
    talking.
Move Parliament to the local community centre.
Free ice cream on Thursdays.
There must be another way…
It's not as simple as doomed or redeemed.
What does 'saving' something actually mean?
Do-gooders, come clean:
Is the world really worth saving?
Time to do something, time is fading.
Stop the clock, do something amazing.

The best hope I've heard
Is to say, '*We* saved the world.'
The end is close, I fear the worst.
Before we save the world,
Let's save humanity first.

BETTER WORLD

Dear Past Henry,

Do you remember, in 2012, you took your solo show to the Edinburgh Fringe? It was called *Letter to the Man (from the boy)*, and you performed poems about growing up. The audience were also invited to join you in writing a letter to their future selves, like a time capsule full of advice and memories.

Do you remember sitting in Underbelly Bar one afternoon, and a producer from another company said to you that she would rather write a letter to her past self? You politely pointed out this was impossible, and defeated the object of the practical show.

Well, guess what? In the year 2088, they found a way to email ourselves in the past. Don't worry about the science. You never were very good at maths.

That's right, you're a hundred years old, and 1988 is considered a vintage year; films of that era, like *Who Framed Roger Rabbit*, are now timeless classics. The Stone Roses are still on tour; admittedly most of the band are cyborgs. Ed Miliband has been voted the greatest peacetime prime minister. Nah, just kidding

Hello. I'm you from the future. The reason I'm emailing is, well, I've been chatting to your grandchildren (yes, it surprised me too).

It started last night. I was watched *The Lady's Got Talent*. It's a reality show where clones of Margaret Thatcher have to compete before a panel of judges.

As a result, I have spent all morning gorging myself on nostalgia, playing punk music on the holographic stereo. Now I've gone really retro, with some classic Bruce Springsteen beamed into my ears using the high-tech photon-nucleus rays. My grandchildren shudder, say I listen to old music. I say, eyes glinting, 'The Boss isn't old; he's vintage!'

They ask me to say something true. They've been having trouble sleeping lately, and want a decent dose of reality. Thanks to the DreamWave advertising programme, each night as they close their eyes and sink into sleep at home, a series of low-density waves beam commercials straight into their parietal lobe. Like gentle, passive ballerinas, advertisements dance across their brains. They never wake up in pain, but they spend mornings in a daze, grazing on food sleepily, sheep-like and quiet. They're finding it hard to tell the difference between reality and the fictions from this brain billboard cold call.

They have tried to complain to the company, but the call centre is manned by a series of cleverly designed Shift Programmes sprites which send calls into a divisional loop system, making it mathematically impossible to reach a human being.

They want a solid, single truth. I jokingly tell them 2 + 2 = 4, and they tell me that was revealed false by the Cognitive Calculation Coalition using the University of Peru's uber-computer. The holo-stereo registers my moodshift and clicks over to playing the chronologically premastered version of the Clash's *London Calling*, where Elvis Presley sings backing vocals on 'Guns of Brixton' and Tom Morello is on guitar for 'Rudie Can't Fail'.

'You want to hear something true?' I establish. They nod, and close the curtains tight with delicate care. I pay a fortune for the curtain tax, so may as well use them when we can. They come sit comfortably on the old sofa. I pour the Fair Trade cider made by starving farmers in Somerset. I telepathically put on my favourite song from the old days, 'Bloody Revolution' by Justin Bieber from his political phase.

I tell them how, in my day, we arranged protests using Twitter accounts, and they say, 'Tw-what?' I tell them how we made online petitions and people from across the globe would sign from the comfort of their own homes. They say, 'Why didn't everyone just use a teleport tube?' I tell them how we couldn't trust our politicians, and they say, 'Why didn't you just inject them with truth toxins?' I tell them how we shared articles and read blogs online to educate ourselves. They wish they had an education, but can't afford the Red Brick chips.

Dear Past Henry.

This world is not how you imagined. It's the world after the future. A post-Jetsons compromise.

Soaked in the wide-eyed expectations of 1950s sci-fi comics, they predicted the future world would be bright, metallic and an everlasting dynasty. A world of automated happiness pumped through our goods and services. They predicted science would be a saviour, defeat all manners of hunger and convert warfare to pleasure, liberate our mental states and free us from mundane tasks. We would meet intelligent life from another planet, and be on its level. And if we looked up, we would see rocket ships, hoverboards and flying cars in the sky. The horizon would be a traffic jam of products.

They predicted a jetpack for every family. Predicted we'd holiday on the moon. They predicted wars would be fought with robots and clones. They predicted we'd conquer space, conquer time travel, conquer our enemies using only justice and truth, and sooner or later we'd discover the secret to eternal youth. They said there'd be snow at Christmas and sun in summer.

But the world we inherited was built with cream plastics, fibre optics and neon. We were handed a world that twanged when touched, a world that could be melted or tarmacked over. A world where a butterfly is an event. A world where atmospheric fog is replaced by practical waves: internet, radio, nuclear and psionic. A trip to the seaside involves a permit, and visiting a local greengrocer's is too much effort. A world where we forgot the recipe for a Sunday dinner.

You just can't give iPods away any more. At car boot sales, they're 20p or six for a pound.

We do not have colonies on the moon, though there are plans for a prison camp on Mars. Have you scanned your Nectar card?

We do not have a cure for HIV and AIDS, though some churches are happy this way. Unexpected item in the bagging tray.

We do not have superheroes flying overhead with X-ray vision, but police can see into your homes with the flick of a switch. Do you want extra fries with this?

We have not yet turned the Green Berets into a Cosmos Division, but, obviously, we still have borders across the world. Your call is important to us, please hold.

We have not yet resurrected Beethoven to finish his symphony, though we still value profit above art. Error. Please restart.

So I'm not sure what to tell my grandchild. Your grandchildren. Because facts are a perfection. In 2088, *perfection* is an archaic word.

I have learnt we were betrayed by possibilities. A prediction is not a promise. Both are loaded, both are dangerous. But we made predictions lightly and placed faith in science to achieve them, and leaders to distribute them.

What about our predictions? We wanted a world without traffic jams. We wanted a world without library fines. We wanted a world without extinction lists. No doomsday clocks, electric chairs, UCAS points, or rejection letters.

I say to my grandchildren, 'So let's take the harder route to the new. Let's make promises. And let's keep them.'

So I love my grandchildren. But I'm sick of predictions, possibilities and failed perfections. I want promises.

Do what I'm doing. Pull out your iPod. Mine is cracked and almost obsolete and dusty.

Play yourself a song written by an old, old friend called Woody Guthrie.

There's a better world a-comin'.

All the best for the future.

Yours sincerely,
Future Henry

(P.S. If you get the chance, Joe Strummer becomes a zombie, so seeing him live in concert is worth every penny.)

THANKS & ACKNOWLEDGEMENTS

Thanks to Mum & Dad, the Say Owt Crew and everyone I've moshed with, marched alongside and lost at Board Games to.